TAKEN BY THE WIND
Vanishing Architecture of the West

TAKEN BY THE WIND
Vanishing Architecture of the West

Ronald Woodall   T. H. Watkins

New York Graphic Society

BOSTON, MASSACHUSETTS

1. Batoche, Saskatchewan (overleaf).

International Standard Book Number: 0-8212-0709-1
Library of Congress Catalog Card Number: 77-77332

First published in Canada by General Publishing Co. Limited
First United States edition

Design/Peter Maher and Ronald Woodall
Editor/Marion E. Raycheba
Research Assistant/Heather Woodall

New York Graphic Society books are published by Little, Brown
and Company.

Printed and bound in U.S.A.
1 2 3 4 5   RRD   81 80 79 78 77

Forewords

This book began one cold spring morning over a decade ago. Standing alone in the absolute silence of a mining ghost town, I felt a shiver run through my bones. Before me was an empty street of forlorn, long-abandoned, useless old wooden buildings. The realization of their exquisite beauty and fragile impermanence struck me with what seemed a very private vision. And so began a long and costly affair, which would, like all obsessive romances, bring moments of great exhilaration and pleasure tempered with painful frustration and deep sadness.

Abandoned country buildings are monuments to laughter and grief and childbirth and death and the best and worst of times. More than that, they are beautiful, not simply because they are old and weathered and picturesque and quaint, but also because they embody the spirit of a noble and resourceful lifestyle. There is intrinsic beauty in functional simplicity and craftsmanship that outlasts the craftsman. There is beauty in timelessness.

The structures in these photographs were probably hand-built by men whose business was not construction or architecture, but farming or mining or merchandising. It seems a minor miracle that they were such fine designers and craftsmen. Perhaps the answer lies in their intent. They built for soundness and endurance. They worked simply, diligently, and resourcefully. They built their buildings to complement an honest and basic lifestyle and, in their innocence, they produced masterpieces.

My dream, as I travel along the West's back roads, is always to find the building that is at one with the land, that has surrendered to the elements. It is not an intruder on the landscape; it is part of it. It has fused with the earth, capitulated to the wind, bent and bowed with the snows, and camouflaged itself with a coating of age. It is gaunt and dry-boned like a great ghost galleon sinking into a grassy sea. It holds secrets and mysteries. It is bizarre. It is elegant. It is chilling. It is enchanting. It is entrancing. It is the grand, magnificent derelict. And the West is a vast repository of these enigmatic artifacts.

The phenomenon of abandonment is, perhaps, unique to the North American West. For any number of reasons, people have simply walked away from their homes and their farms, sometimes leaving entire cities and towns empty. The buildings that remain, structures erected by simple people with simple tools for simple, functional reasons, were highly personal undertakings and the result is high folk sculpture.

Actually, it is remarkable that this book could have been done at all. I started too late. The best of the old West is gone. It was gone before I began. Herein lies the frustration and sadness. A good third of the buildings in this book have already disappeared. Another third will likely disappear in the 1980s. The back country is succumbing to future shock,

and every year my travels become more heartbreaking.

These simple country buildings cannot be saved. They cannot be refinished like a spinning wheel for some suburban living room. They cannot be towed to a garage for restoration like a vintage car. They cannot justify the space they take and no law can protect them. And that is sad.

Ronald Woodall
June 1977

The North American West: Surely the hand of God could not have created a broader and more diverse landscape for the absurd, the venal, the fierce, the noble, or the tragic adventures of man. It is roughly split by the jumble of mountains called the Rockies, the twisting, spiny backbone of the continent that stretches from Mexico to the northwesternmost of Canada's Northwest Territories. To the east of this wandering upthrust lie a series of grassy, gently overlapping plains that flow from the Peace River country of Alberta to the panhandle of Texas. Though not dry enough to be called desert, this great tongue of land averages twenty inches or fewer of rainfall every year, which gives it a condition of semi-aridity. The true deserts lie to the west of the Rockies in wrinkled pockets and bowls and basins scattered from southern New Mexico and Arizona to eastern Oregon and Washington. These are definitive wastelands, from the Biblical ruin of Death Valley in California to the scrubby high desert of eastern Oregon. Paradoxically, in a region dominated by the aridity of its plains and deserts, the snow fountains of its mountain ranges—not only the Rockies, but also such others as the Wasatch, the Brooks, the Alaskan, the Cascades, the Sierra Nevada—feed some of the greatest rivers in the western hemisphere: the Yukon, the Mackenzie, the Peace, the Saskatchewan, the Columbia, the Missouri, the Yellowstone, the Platte, the Snake, the Green, the Colorado, the Sacramento, the Rio Grande. Cutting through the plateaus and the mountains in the course of fulfilling their task of tearing down the land and carrying it into the sea, these rivers have carved some of the deepest wounds on the face of the planet: Hells Canyon of the Snake River, the Grand Canyon of the Yellowstone, the Grand Canyon of the Colorado, the Gorge of the Rio Grande.

Three million square miles of mountains, deserts, plains, rivers, and canyons, infinitely various in all its parts—but it is not merely the sheer grandeur of this landscape that seduces our attention and captures our imagination. For European men—men of our own kind and character—have been at work in this land for more than four centuries and in the process have assembled a body of myth, legend, experience, and history that is the common inheritance of two nations: Canada and the United States.

It was a parade, a noisy, bustling, vigorous pageant that expressed the human animal at his best and at his worst, and all the shades between. The people who first met and conquered this wilderness carried with them a fierce vision like a fire in the heart, one expressed with an equally fierce eloquence by United States Congressman Galusha A. Grow in 1852: "The achievements of your pioneer army, from the day that they first drove back the Indian tribes from your Atlantic seaboard to the present hour, have been the achievements of science and civilization over the elements, the wilderness, and the savage. The settler, in search of a new home, long since o'erlapped the Alleghanies, and, having crossed the great central valley of the Mississippi, is now wending his way to the shores of the Pacific; the forest stoops to allow the emigrant to pass; and the wilderness gives way to the tide of emigration....

"During the two and a quarter centuries since Jamestown and Plymouth Rock were consecrated by the exile, trace the footsteps of the pioneer, as he has gone forth to...build up new empires. In these two and a quarter centuries, from an unbroken forest, you have a country embracing almost every variety of production, and extending through almost every zone. The high regions of the North have scarcely thrown off their icy mantle, while the Southern reaper is preparing for his harvest home. The morning sun tips your eastern hills, while the valleys of the West repose in midnight darkness. In these two and a quarter centuries, a whole continent has been converted to the use of man, and upon its bosom has arisen the noblest empire on earth."

Once upon a time. We can today deplore the bumptious arrogance of such words, knowing as we do with the splendid wisdom of hindsight that there was a good deal more than nobility involved in the conquest of the West. We know that when the Iron Age met the Stone Age it was not we who were the victims, but those Indian peoples who had inhabited this continent for thousands of years before there was any such thing as European civilization. We know that the West was quite as often raped of its resources as it was blessed with the trappings of our unique culture. We know, too, that for many—perhaps most—of those who entered the wilderness the experience ended in exhaustion, despair, even death. We know, finally, because we can look around us at the evidence, that whatever was good in the vision that led our people to cross the mountains and the deserts for a new life has long since succumbed to the pressures of an age which has little time for the creation of new and presumably better lives. We have, we suspect, betrayed something, possibly something important. We could call it hope, or we

could, like a character in John Steinbeck's **The Red Pony**, call it something else: "Westering has died out of the people. Westering isn't a hunger any more. It's done."

Westering and all that it meant is done, and most of those who would have understood its meaning are no longer with us—nor is much of the civilization they struggled so long and hard to impose on the wilderness. Neither should be forgotten, for both have shaped our history, and an understanding of history is one of the tools necessary to the maintenance of a living society. That understanding is the main purpose of this book. In its own modest way, it seeks to achieve the stature of a document—truth as an exercise of the imagination. The essays and commentaries scattered through **Taken by the Wind** do not stand as a formal history, nor are they meant to; they seek to establish how close we are to those who came before us and how much it is we owe them. The photographs make their own, separate statement, for they portray the very artifacts which those who came before us left behind them. Like the archeologist's sand-screen, the eye of Ronald Woodall has sifted through the detritus of a way of life and has captured on film its essential images—the bones and shards and splinters out of which we can reconstruct the physical and emotional life of a time and a people now taken by the wind.

T. H. Watkins
June 1977

Contents

The Pioneers

"...driven by an
insane desire to better
their condition in life...."

After more than a century of exposure through books and, later, motion pictures and television, the pioneer experience has become something of an historical cliché. We think we know what it was all about, for the images come to us so readily: the long line of white-topped wagons creeping across a stretch of prairie or being hauled up the slope of a mountain pass or pulled into a circle for protection against marauding Indians; the Indians themselves surrounding the wagons, galloping in furious attack, the settlers huddled behind boxes and barrels, firing desperately, surely soon to be overcome, but never are; the faces of both men and women, taut, grim, determined, burned by wind and sun, forever brave; pioneers....

The trouble with such images, of course, is that they mix fact and fancy so completely that it is nigh impossible to get at the reality behind them. This is true even for the Canadian West, which had no wagon-train pioneers to speak of; the earliest settlers of the far West in Canada were Métis from the Red River, and they came not in wagons, but in ox-carts—and most of the later settlers came on the cars of the Canadian Pacific and Great Northern railroads. Nevertheless, it is important to try to get behind such images, for there really were men and women who endured the sometimes incredible hardships of the trek west [though only very, very rarely did these hardships include Indian attacks; for the most part, the Indians were content to slip in and steal cattle and horses when they could]. And what they did was a truly astonishing thing; with an admirable if frequently naive tenacity, they leaped over more than two thousand miles of territory to pin civilization down, finally, at both ends of the continent. Too noteworthy an achievement to be left to the mercies of the myth-makers.

Let us consider, then, the first ones. They were the true pioneers, for their experiences established a pattern for those who came after; the trails they found and sometimes broke became the roads of an entire generation.

Their motivations, for the most part, were simple enough. They were "driven," as the haughty Boston Brahmin Francis Parkman described it somewhat contemptuously, "by an insane desire to better their condition in life," which in their view included free land in a new country. Their backgrounds were similar: generally Anglo-Saxon, piously Protestant, and of what might be called the rural middle-class; if not well-off, they were at least in comfortable circumstances, for it took money, quite a bit of money, for a family to outfit itself with equipment, provisions, and animals, and truly poor people were a rare sight on the western trails. Among them, they shared the same qualities of greed, nobility, selfishness, generosity, bravery, and cowardice that might be expected of any collection of human beings anywhere; at the same time, they would not have been reluctant to include themselves in the idealized description given their kind by Henry Clay in 1842:

"Pioneers," he said, "penetrate into the uninhabited regions of the West. They apply the axe to the forest, which falls before them, or the plough to the prairie, deeply sinking its share in the unbroken wild grasses in which it abounds. They build houses, plant orchards, enclose fields, cultivate the earth, and raise up families around them." Their desire to do just that bemused mountain man James Clyman, who encountered many of them in 1846: "It is remarkable," he wrote in his diary, "that so many of all kinds and classes of People should sell out comfortable homes in Missouri and Elsewhere pack up and start across such an emmence Barren waste to settle in some new Place of which they have at most so uncertain information but this is the character of my countrymen."

It was indeed, and in the 1830s and 1840s Clyman's countrymen began exercising their characters on an increasingly enthusiastic scale. The places of which they had "at most so uncertain information" were Oregon and California, places, as a combination of slim fact, rumor, and wishful thinking had it, where a man could not only sustain his life on the land but also prosper upon it, freed of the bitter eastern winters and allowed to expand his farmland, his crops, and his possiblities as far as he might care to take them.

But first they had to get there, no simple proposition. They came into the outfitting and "jumping-off" towns on the Missouri River—chiefly Council Bluffs, Iowa, and St. Joseph and Independence, Missouri—from all over the east, but most from the nearby states of Missouri, Iowa, and Illinois. Most brought their own wagons; others purchased them in the outfitting towns. In either case, they generally overloaded them, often with such reminders of the homes they had left as spinet pianos, breakfronts, and cases of family china, most of it sooner or later abandoned on the trail. If they had not already organized themselves into individual trains in their home states, they did so now, sometimes with painstaking "constitutions," sometimes with a splendid informality. They elected themselves a captain for the train, a position that had then all the tenure of that of a baseball manager today, for this was democracy on the move, and if a man did not come up to what his neighbors expected of him, he would frequently find himself ousted somewhere along the trail by a vote of no confidence and a quick replacement.

After stocking up with provisions and additional oxen, cattle, and horses, a train would gather itself together one fine spring morning and cross the wide Missouri, then follow it north [or, in the case of Council Bluffs, south] to the mouth of the Platte River and turn west toward the Rocky Mountains. This was the beginning of what came to be known as the California-Oregon Trail. With few variations, the route followed the valley of the Platte to Fort Laramie, from there through the wide and gradual incline called South Pass —which cut across the continental divide—across the Green River to Fort

Bridger, then northwest to Fort Hall on the Snake River. Here, the trail divided. Those bound for Oregon continued northwest along the Snake River Plains to Fort Boise, north from there to the headwaters of the Columbia River, west across the Cascades, then down the Columbia to Fort Vancouver near its mouth before spilling out into the countryside to settle. Those bound for California moved southwest from Fort Hall, crossed the northern reaches of the Salt Desert to the Humboldt [then Mary's] River, down that to its sink, went across the Truckee Desert to the Truckee River, then up either its canyons or those of the Carson River farther south to cross the Sierra Nevada over Donner or Walker passes, and finally stumbled down out of the mountains to the golden valley of California's Sacramento River.

To contemplate such routes today, nearly a century and a half since, is easily enough done. Encapsulated in our steel and aluminum and plastic vehicles, slipping without effort along the smooth highways, they mean little to us: a few rivers, a few canyons, a few mountains, a few deserts. But to the pioneers, the simple act of getting from one place to the other was a task of almost superhuman effort, of daily, creeping progress, of sheer toil of a dimension that staggers the imagination, of constant exposure to heat, cold, wind, rain, flies, and dust, of a stultifying boredom interrupted only by long periods of work or moments of terror. To read the journals from that time — and a remarkable number of travelers somehow found the energy to keep them — is to experience an almost constant litany of difficulty. Wagons broke down and had to be repaired. Oxen, cattle, and horses mired in buffalo wallows and mysterious unexpected bogs or were swept away while fording rivers. Crude rafts had to be fashioned to carry everybody and everything across rivers that could not be forded. Water would be plentiful for one week and practically nonexistent for another three. Forage for the animals would decline to stubby un-nourishing clumps or, in the desert crossings, disappear altogether. Game, such as buffalo and antelope, was bountiful east of Fort Laramie, but west of that post steadily deteriorated until it was fruitless to spend the time looking for it. Dysentery wracked just about everyone at one time or another, and vague fevers left others helpless for weeks. Minor injuries hampered many and serious injuries crippled others. To ascend in many places took days of tedious labor, hitching as many as twelve yoke of oxen to a single wagon and inching it to the top, then, assuming it had not backslid, reversing the process and inching it down the other slope. For week after week, for as much as four or five months, the dull, steady, mind-numbing work went on, and over it all hung the need to press on, press on, to get to the last mountains between them and their goal before the snows of winter trapped them in this harsh, inchoate country. Those who survived came into their new land in a state of physical and emotional exhaustion, and it is a tribute to the sheer resiliency of the spirit and flesh of these people that there was anything left in them once they arrived to "build houses, plant orchards, enclose fields, cultivate the earth, and rear up families around them."

And, of course, there were those who did not survive, for death was a commonplace on the trail. There is virtually no account of the trips of these early overlanders that does not include at least one death, and in most cases several. Most were the result of accident or disease; very few deaths occurred in violent confrontations, including conflict with Indians. Some shot themselves accidentally; some drowned; some died in wagon accidents; and some merely slipped away, wasted by exhaustion and disease, as did two relatives of Nicholas Carriger, who had finally pulled his way over the Sierra Nevada only to record surely one of the most moving passages in the annals of the western migration: "After climbing the steep mountain we kept on travelling without meeting any accidents, till the evening of the 26th of september 1846 when I had the misfortune of loosing my father and sister in law, both having been called to their long home about at the same hour; and strange as it may seem the same hour in which my respected father expired, my beloved wife gave birth to a lively little girl.... I placed the dead bodies of my relatives in a wagon, handsomely decorated with black crepe, and at night having reached the fords of the Yuba river I there dug two graves and consigned their beloved remains to mother earth...."

The shadow of ruin was never far from the minds of these hardy, matter-of-fact people, and even more so after the winter of 1846-47. For this was the winter of the Donner Party, whose memory the West has carried like a fire in the heart and whose story, even briefly told, stands as a dark parable for the entire pioneer experience. The party's members, numbering eighty-seven men, women, and children, had, like the rest of the approximately twenty-seven hundred emigrants to Oregon and California that year, started out with the best and bravest of hopes. Unfortunately, they left a bit later than most that year, had unforeseen delays along the way, and by the time they reached Fort Bridger, it was near the end of July. They would have to hurry to make it across the Sierra Nevada into California before winter. At this juncture, the party decided to take a new, shorter route rumored to save several weeks of travel; instead of heading north to Fort Hall, then southwest to the Humboldt River, it would cut more directly west straight through the canyon of the Weber River in the Wasatch Mountains of Utah, from there cross the desert south of the Great Salt Lake, then meet the Humboldt at a point many miles below the normal route. But rumor did it in; it took weeks for the party to clamber through the mountains to the Great Salt Lake and more weeks of desperate struggle before the Humbolt was reached. By the time the party had found the Truckee River it had already witnessed snow flurries. It was not until the end of October that the emigrants reached Truckee [now Donner] Lake some two thousand feet below the summit of the mountains. Before they could gather their energy to assault this last barrier, it began to snow and did so for eight straight days. They were trapped.

When the snow let up briefly, rude shelters were constructed to house the bulk of the party while a picked handful somehow made it over the pass to find food and rescuers. Those who stayed behind saw no one from across the pass for more than two months. Those rescuers who were finally able to get across the drifts of one of the worst winters in the history of the mountains on February 18, 1847, found an unimaginable charnel-house. Driven almost mindless by hunger, many of those who had survived that winter had done so on the flesh of dead relatives and friends. In the end, forty-five of the original eighty-seven members of the party had died.

Horror? Yes, and one would not like to share the nightmares of those who had succumbed to the lust of hunger. The Donner Party tragedy places a grisly pall over the history of the westward movement, yet even out of that dreadful experience the survivors carried with them into California the same tough dream of hope that had energized all those who first decided to find a new definition of their lives in another land, that had enabled them to muscle their way through more hardship over a longer period of time than anything the present generation will ever know, that would sustain them as they built a new society where none had ever been before. Young Virginia Reed had that hope. Only thirteen years old when the rescuers dug her out of the snow of Donner Lake, she had lived through and seen it all. And on her way down the mountain she received her first marriage proposal. Some days later, she wrote a cousin back in Illinois: "Tell the girls that this is the greatest place for marrying they ever saw...."

Pioneers. We will not see their like again.

With the Materials at Hand...

The ingenuity of the pioneer settler was one of his most celebrated virtues—as well as a matter of the plainest necessity. In a land and time devoid of the most common amenities we take for granted today, a man did what he could with what he had and, more often than not, did it with his own hands. Nowhere was this reflected more consistently than in the homes and other structures put together with the materials and tools at hand, whether logs, as in the stage stop and ranch near the Cariboo goldfields of British Columbia [4] or the ancient adobe of Taos Pueblo in New Mexico [5]. In between, mud, stone, straw, natural lime mortar, and the most primitive material of them all—plain sod.

3. Slate wall in Bear Valley, California.

8. Reconstructed sod house, Duck Lake, Saskatchewan.

4. Dovetailed logs at 108-Mile House, British Columbia.

5. Adobe wall, Taos, New Mexico.

6. Mud-brick and straw shed near Hilda, Alberta.

7. Mud and stone barn, Burstall, Saskatchewan.

10. General store in Lee's Corners, British Columbia.

9. "Stove log" barn, Gimli, Manitoba (overleaf).

Form, function, and simplicity. . . . Part of the charm of handmade houses and other structures in the West is their very crudity. Designed to fulfill very specific functions, each nonetheless was marked by the personality of the builder in an individual way and few of them are exactly alike any other. An interesting example is the original general store of Lee's Corners, British Columbia [10]. Others are a barn on the Alkali Lake Ranch of British Columbia [11] and one near Hydraulic, also British Columbia [12].

11. Barn, Alkali Lake Ranch, British Columbia.

12. Barn, Hydraulic, British Columbia.

13. Reconstructed log wall, Molson, Washington.

14. Edwards barn, Kersley, British Columbia.

15. Barn near Buffalo, Wyoming.

16. Storefront in Bannack, Montana.

The Farms and Ranches

"The government bets 160 acres
against the entry fee...that
the settler can't live on the land
for five years without
starving to death."

Summer 1874, the Great Plains: Everyone suspected they would be coming; no one expected it to be so bad. The sky was alive with them, the ground moved like a living carpet of billions upon billions of insects. It was the first of four summers of an almost Biblical locust plague that would strike much of the West from Manitoba to Texas, from the Rockies to the Mississippi, destroying no one ever knew how much vegetation, eating no one ever knew how many crops. "Such a bunch of insects I never saw," a Kansas homesteader wrote. "The ground is completely covered and the branches of the trees are bending down with their weight. In my orchard of nearly twenty acres the trees are covered by myriads. The grove on the north is one huge, moving mass. Thirty acres of wheat that looked beautiful and green in the morning is eaten up. Six hundred and forty acres, two miles south of me, that was looking fine in the beginning of the week, looks this morning as though fire had passed over it." A reporter from the St. Louis **Republican** was equally appalled: "A glance upward toward the sun revealed them filling the air as far as vision could extend, as thick as snowflakes in a storm, and they drifted along with the breeze, and fluttered down at your feet occasionally or lit on your nose, with as much unconcern as if they had been part of the elements." Railroad locomotives had to pour sand on their tracks for enough traction to move over the crushed and oily bodies of grasshoppers. Nothing would stop them, not fire or kerosene or poisons, and again they came in ever-increasing multitudes in the summer of 1875, of 1876, of 1877. They never came again in such numbers, and to this day no one knows precisely why.

Early fall 1886, the Great Plains: The narrator is John Clay, co-owner of the VVV Ranch on the Wind River of Montana: "By August, it was hot, dry, dusty and grass closely cropped. Every day made it apparent that even with the best of winters cattle would have a hard time and 'through' cattle would only winter with a big percentage of loss.... Our neighbors kept piling cattle onto the bone dry range. The Continental Cattle Co., with no former hold-ings turned loose 5,000 head or thereabouts. Major Smith, who had failed to sell 5,500 southern three-year-old steers, was forced to drive them to his range on Willow Creek.... The Dickey Cattle Co...had brought up 6,000 mixed cattle from the Cheyenne and Arapahoe country and turned them over to their outfit whose headquarters were twenty or twenty-five miles below [Alzada] on the little Missouri. Thousands of other cattle were spread over the western and northwestern country in the most reckless way, no thought for the morrow...."

The "morrow" was winter, one of the longest and deadliest in the history of the West. And in the spring of 1887, the rotting piles of dead cattle were stacked like cordwood in the corners of barbed-wire fences. Their bloated, fly-ridden bodies clogged and poisoned the Yellowstone, Powder, Belle Fourche, and Platte Rivers, cluttered gullies and gulches, littered the road-sides, and the stink of carrion hung in the air like swamp fog for weeks. "It was simply appalling," Clay wrote, "and the cowmen could not realize their position. From southern Colorado to the Canadian line, from the 100th Meridian almost to the Pacific Slope it was a catastrophe.... Three great streams of ill-luck, mismanagement, greed, met together. In other words, recklessness, want of foresight, and the weather, which no man can control."

The Great Plains was not a land that took kindly to the efforts of men to put it to their own uses, as the examples cited above suggest. If farming and ranching are games of chance and farmers and ranchers gamblers, then nowhere were the odds against success stacked higher than in the country that lay between the ninety-eighth meridian and the Rockies, sweeping in a northwestern curve from just above Texas to the Canadian line and through Manitoba, Saskatchewan, and Alberta. Farming and ranching in the West did not begin in this land, of course; the lush valleys of Oregon first tasted the blade of the plow in the 1840s and the San Joaquin Valley of California was rapidly becoming a major wheat producer in the 1850s; similarly, the rolling hills of the California coast had provided the graze for thousands of cattle long before the first transMississippi settlers set foot on the plains. But it was here, on these North American steppes, that the game was played out on its broadest scale and the contest between man and land was most profound.

Some won, and won big—for a time. Take, for example, the wheat bonanza in the Red River Valley in the 1870s and early 1880s. This valley, twenty to forty miles wide, stretches some three hundred miles south from Lake Winnipeg in Manitoba through Minnesota and the Dakotas; its potential was outlined by a writer for the **Cultivator and Country Gentleman** of 1877: "The surface of the land is nearly level, with but sufficient undulation to afford good drainage; the soil a rich, friable, black alluvial mold some thirty inches deep...and almost every acre can be put under the plow in unbroken furrows from one to the other." Almost every acre was, as a matter of fact. In 1875, the Northern Pacific Railroad, which owned much of the valley through government grants, decided to demonstrate its richness to stimulate land sales to settlers. The company put some eighteen sections of its Red River land in the hands of Oliver Dalrymple, an experienced wheat grower from Minnesota, gave him enough money for seed, equipment, animals, and labor, and told him to make it grow; his reward would be half of each farm he developed once the company got its investment [with interest] back. Dalrymple made it grow. The first season's crop yielded a remarkable average of twenty-three bushels an acre, a figure the company leaped upon and broadcast to the world. The boom that followed, like most such booms in the West, was largely a corporate matter, and only rarely did a lucky independent invest his flimsy resources and come out of the whole business intact—much less as a winner. But for those with adequate resources, the Red River bonanza paid off most handsomely. The cost per acre of bringing in a crop was rarely more than ten dollars; that acre would yield anywhere from twenty to twenty-four bushels at an average sale price during the boom years of ninety cents each. Impressive figures, those, and the farms—most of them owned by easterners and put in the hands of managers—expanded to incredible sizes: The Grandin Farms, 61,100 acres; the Dalrymple Farms, 100,000 acres; the Hillsboro Farm, 40,000 acres; the Cooper Farms, 34,000 acres; the Amenia and Sharon Land Company, 28,350 acres; the Spiritwood Farms, 19,700 acres; the Mosher Farms, 19,000 acres; and overall, the **average** bonanza farm was 7,000 acres. They were less farms than factories; armies of laborers sweated out the crop with the aid of great, rattling, clanking machines—plows and harvesters and threshers and combines.

And then it dribbled away. Beginning in 1885, wheat prices steadily declined all the way to the end of the century; the seasons became more dry, producing thinner crops; taxes rose higher and higher. By the middle of the 1890s, most of the great bonanza farms had folded up, and the West would not see another such boom until the years of World War I and the 1920s, when the bonanza farms [these, too, short-lived] moved farther northwest to Montana and southern Saskatchewan and Alberta, clear up to the Peace River country of the north.

The range cattle industry followed a remarkably similar pattern of boom and bust in the same period. While the driving of Texas cattle to northern [and occasionally, Californian] markets had been fairly common in the 1850s, it was not until after the Civil War that the business began to give hints of the boom to come. In 1866, some 260,000 head of longhorns were driven north; the numbers fell off during the next two years, but rose to 350,000 in 1869 and to a never-again equalled 600,000 in 1871. The railroads moving west met the cows heading north, and at the meeting points the great cowtowns of legend sprang up—Wichita, Abilene, Newton, Ellsworth, Caldwell, and the greatest of them all, Dodge City. Yet by the mid-1870s the emphasis of the industry began to shift from Texas to the northern plains, whose rich grasses provided superior graze on which to fatten the cattle for market. Soon, as many cattle were being driven to Colorado, Wyoming, Nebraska, Montana, and the Dakotas as to the Kansas shipping points. They fed and fattened on buffalo grass; were bred and rebred until the leathery meat of the Texas longhorns was replaced by the tender flesh of the shorthorn; and by 1880 much of the northern plains from Alberta and Saskatchewan to Wyoming and Colorado had been converted into an immense pasture; estimates, while loose, give the possible number of animals at nearly two million.

As in the wheat bonanza of the Red River Valley, the boom years of the cattle industry were dominated by investment capital—most of it from the east and much of it from foreign lands. The largest ranches, like the bonanza farms, were put in the control of managers, and often the only direct contact the owners had with their ranches—running in size to the scores of thousands of acres—were when they used them as headquarters for their summer hunting jaunts. Unlike the bonanza wheat industry, however, the cattle industry nurtured the existence of one of the best-known and least-understood creatures ever to inhabit the West: the cowboy. In what historian W. H. Hutchinson has dubbed our "thud-and-blunder" tradition, we have so shrouded the cowboy in a cottony smother of legend that one has to go out of one's way to learn anything real about him. He was a workman, the "hired hand on horseback," and probably the hardest-working of all workmen in the West. He worked from sunup to sundown, six and often seven days a week, and did it for thirty dollars a month and bunkhouse privileges. He lived and worked daily with two of the most recalcitrant, ill-tempered, and perverse animals on the face of the earth: the horse and the cow. "Every horse," cowboy-historian-philosopher Owen Ulph has written, "should be branded with a swastika," and of the personality flaws of the cow he was only a little less eloquent: "So uncanny is the intuition of the cow that it can almost always sense what the rider wants it to do, and do the opposite." What the cowboy got out of all this—aside from a social standing that put him only a little above the cow in the standards of his day—was not much, but for him enough: the raw nerve that he called "gumption," a gnarled and wiry independence, and that true sense of his own worth that can only come to a man who has combined stoicism and humor to make a shield against adversity. If the cowboy was a hero, it was not because of any blazing six-gun adventures, but because he endured what other men could not have endured.

But the great days of the cowboy, like those of his industry, were numbered. Greed, together with an almost total ignorance of what the land could reasonably hold, led ranch owners to order more and more cattle on to their ranges. Then came a drought in the spring and summer of 1886; grass as well as water was badly depleted, leaving the cattle in poor shape for the winter. And that winter was one of the worst in memory. The results were predictably grisly: in the "Big Die-up" of 1886-87 hundreds of thousands of cattle perished, ruining scores of large and small ranchers and putting the industry into a decline from which it did not fully recover for nearly a generation.

In the end, of course, despite the flash and flurry of the boom years in wheat and cattle, those who made the most permanent mark on the face of the Great Plains were those who gained the least and had the most to lose. They were the family farmers—though just as often known as sod-busters, homesteaders, or, in the view of irritated cattlemen, nesters.

Their presence on this land was no random accident. In 1862, the Congress of the United States passed the Homestead Act, which provided that any head of household or person over twenty-one years of age [including aliens who had declared their intention of becoming citizens] had a right to one hundred and sixty acres of government land; full title could be attained after living on the land for five years, by improving it with the building of a house or by cultivating it, and by the payment of a small entry fee. In 1872, after it purchased from the Hudson's Bay Company—for $1,500,000—all western land which the company had erroneously declared "unfit for settlement," the Canadian government provided its own homestead law in the Dominion Land Act; the only appreciable difference between the two acts was that the Dominion Land Act required but three years of residence.

Free land, or almost free, and well-nigh irresistable. In the United States, 552,112 homestead entries were made between 1862 and 1882. Canada lagged behind considerably, but between 1872 and 1900, some 88,000 entries had been made, and by 1905, because of the vigorous proselytizing efforts of the Hon. Clifford Sutton, the minister in charge of populating the country's western lands, an estimated five million acres of homestead lands were under cultivation. In addition to homestead lands were railroad lands. As the Canadian Pacific, the Northern Pacific, the Union Pacific, and the Santa Fe Railroads inched across the continent, they did so with the aid of government grants of land. These lands provided the railroads with a potentially steady source of income through sales, and railroad land agents soon infested the American and Canadian easts, most of the countries of western Europe, and England, Scotland, Wales, and Ireland. They came, the people, and came by the thousands.

Who were they? They were everyone, probably as diverse a collection of nationalities as any given region has ever seen: Irish, Scots, Welsh, English, Germans, Swedes, Norwegians, Danes, French, Ukranians, Galicians, Poles, Ruthenians, Hungarians, Canadians crossing the line into America, and Americans crossing the line into Canada. Whether homesteaders or owners of railroad land, whether Ukrainian or Magyar, they faced a task that was almost impossible. For this was the arid West, a land against which a man could pit his best energies, his experience, and his hope and come out with nothing but the sour taste of failure and humiliation. "The government," United States Senator William E. Borah once commented in regard to the Homestead Act, "bets 160 acres against the entry fee…that the settler can't live on the land for five years without starving to death."

Not many starved, but too many came too close to starvation, and all suffered the vagaries of a climate as unpredictable as it was frequently violent. "The possibilities of trouble, which increased in geometrical ratio beyond the hundredth meridian," Wallace Stegner has written, "had a tendency to multiply in clusters. The brassy sky of drouth might open to let across the fields winds like the breath of a blowtorch, or clouds of grasshoppers, or crawling armies of chinch bugs. Pests always seemed to thrive best in drouth years. And if drouth and insect plagues did not appear there was always a chance of cyclones, cloudbursts, hail.

"It took a man to break and hold a homestead of 160 acres even in the subhumid zone. It took a superman to do it on the arid plains. It could hardly, in fact, be done, though some heroes tried it."

Of the 552,112 homestead entries made in the United States between 1862 and 1882, only 194,488 "proved up" over the five year period of residence, and a similar percentage of failure took place in the Canadian West. Yet there **were** heroes on the land, and if the pious and persevering settlers who somehow managed to hold on to their land, to subsist on it if not necessarily prosper from it, lacked the colorful legends of the cowboy, if they lacked both the resources and the imagination of those entrepreneurs who created and participated in the bonanza booms, they were nevertheless the heart and the future of a new land.

18. Ranch buildings, Eagle Butte, Alberta.

19. Farmhouse, St. Denis, Saskatchewan.

20. Abandoned farmhouse near High River, Alberta.

21. Abandoned farmhouse in Swan Valley, Idaho.

22. Farmhouse near Andrew, Alberta.

23. House and former post office in Langley, British Columbia.

24. Farmhouse near Samish, Washington.

25. Chesaw, Washington.

26. Netherhill, Saskatchewan.

27. Abandoned house, Park City, Utah.

You see such houses all over the West—lost, lonely, decrepit, and almost always deserted. Topping a rise or hunkered down in a hollow, they seem dwarfed by an environment of space, windblown and weathered, twisted and riven by the elements. Their windows are as blank as the eyes of a skull, and, indeed, there is something almost pathetically human about them. That is understandable, for generations have been born in them, lived in them, loved in them, fought, sweat, and died in them. Their very presence reeks of long human habitation; they are constant, living reminders of those who have gone before us. There is something of this in any abandoned house, but more so for these—because these are **farm**houses and because of that each implies a history of hope. One of the oldest dreams of western man—perhaps the oldest—has been that of the individual farmer working the individual plot of land. It was this hope that sent most men to North America in the first place, and it was this hope that sent them—British, Scots, Irish, Swedes and Norwegians, Ukrainians and Americans— across the mountain and river barriers to enter the lands of the West, lands that stretched out until they were lost beyond the horizon. They brought with them hope, sweat, muscle, and determination, and very little else, and most of them lost it all in the face of the too often bitter reality that the land held for them. So if these photographs of abandoned farmhouses seem to carry with them a strange and indefinable poignance, it is because they stand as monuments to failed dreams.

28.   House near Sedro Woolley, Washington.

30. Wood and adobe farmhouse, Brazos, New Mexico.

32. Farmhouse on Douglas Plateau near Pritchard, British Columbia.

33. Hazlet, Saskatchewan.

34. Granite, Oregon.

35. Stephensville, Montana.

36. 108-Mile House, British Columbia.

37. Shackleton, Saskatchewan.

38. Cripple Creek, Colorado.

39. Bannack, Montana.

40. Hill Spring, Alberta.

41. Dairy barn near Jacksonville, Oregon (overleaf).

From Here to There, Then to Now...

"In the old days," historian-novelist Wallace Stegner has written, "in blizzardly weather, we used to tie a string of lariats from house to barn so as to make it from shelter to responsibility and back again. With personal, family, and cultural chores to do, I think we had better rig up such a line between past and present." Stegner spent much of his childhood on the plains of northern Montana and southern Saskatchewan, and both the image he invoked and the conclusion he drew from it were natural outgrowths of that experience. Both, in fact, are in part what this book is about —images of a past whose meaning can enrich our own time. And certainly, few images of that past are more commonly shared than that of the barn. Even if we have never seen or stood in one, we think we know: space and coolness, filtered half-light, the smells of leather, animals, and the ineffable sweetness of hay. For most of us in this urbanized age of concrete and plastic, such barn-memories are acts of pure imagination, but no less valuable for all that. They have their own kind of truth; they are one of Stegner's lines between past and present.

42. North Palouse, Washington.

43. Mount Currie Indian Reserve, British Columbia.

44. Hardman, Oregon.

47. Copperopolis, California.

45. Bayfield, Colorado.

48. Mundare, Alberta.

46. Near Assiniboia, Saskatchewan.

49. Near Superior, Montana.

Barns as Billboards...

There will always be an advertising man. Today, when driving about the West, the kind of advertising you see will more often than not wink and glitter at you in all the variations of neon that human ingenuity can contrive—touting the virtues of gasoline brands, quik-food stops [the spelling is deliberate], motels, and, in Nevada, of course, gambling casinos and other dubious haunts. As the photographs here illustrate, however, there was a time when both the products and the means of advertising them possessed a more homely—and, we will insist, more charming—character. Like the famous roadside ''Burma-Shave'' signs of the 1920s and 1930s, most of the older barnside advertisements have almost completely vanished from the western scene, but once in a while, on a lonely back road here and there, you can still see them, their fading messages like epitaphs to products and purposes long since shoveled into the dustbin of history.

51. Everett, Washington.

52. Waterville, Washington.

50. Ashland, Oregon.

53. Oakland, Oregon.

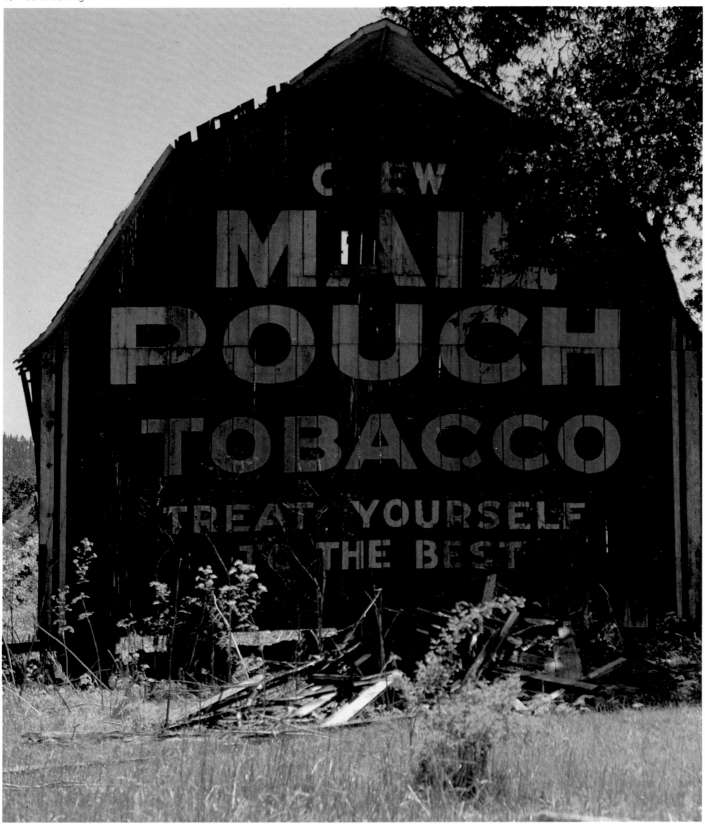

The Round Barn...

Seemingly so esoteric as to have been imported whole from some eastern European rural area, the occasional round barn in the West had a purely practical function: although the amount of materials and expertise required exceeded those of the standard style of western barns, the ability of the round barn to shed snow and withstand wind was much greater—and an additional advantage was greater internal space for animals. For example, the Bartel barn near Drake, Saskatchewan [62] contains 2827 square feet of floor space —651 square feet more than a standard barn with the same length of outside wall.

54. Twin Bridges, Montana.

56. Macdonald, Manitoba.

55. Empress, Alberta.

57. Waterloo, Montana.

61. Steptoe, Washington.

58. Indian Head, Saskatchewan.

59. Fort Edmonton, Alberta.

62. Drake, Saskatchewan.

60. St. John, Washington.

Hop Barns...

Like most "specialty crops" in the West, the growing of hops was—and is—an operation of considerable dimensions, requiring extensive lands, capital investment, and a seasonal labor force of pickers for harvesting. One reminder of that fact is the "Wheatland Riots" of 1913, when local deputies and hired thugs clashed with labor organizers in California's Sacramento Valley; at day's end, four men were dead and several wounded—a singularly telling illustration of the labor strife that too often characterized industrialized agriculture in the West. More gentle reminders of the size and substance of the hop industry were the great barns constructed to store its crops—particularly the massive stone creation [64], a structure near Healdsburg, California, currently under reconstruction.

64. Healdsburg, California.

63. Fulton, California.

65. Wilsonville, Oregon.

Liveries and Stables. . .

While the horse has largely been reduced to a plaything for
weekend cowboys and casual **aficionados** and the mule has
all but disappeared from the scene, both were once essential
tools on the ranches and farms of the West. Until the advent
of steam-powered and later gasoline-powered vehicles—
everything from Jeeps to monstrous tractors—the horse and
the mule provided mobility in a land of immense distance
and the musclepower to make that land pay. Which is not to
say that either animal was universally loved by those who
used them. "A horse," ex-cowboy and motion-picture actor
Tim McCoy has said, "was something you got on and rode."
Others have been less kind, and to many working cowboys
the horse was the meanest-tempered, most contrary, and
most treacherous four-footed creature on the face of the
earth—with the possible exception of the cow. The mule
got hardly a better press, and in **The Reivers**, William
Faulkner explained that one of the reasons was that a mule
"will work for you patiently for ten years for the chance to
kick you once." Whether loved or unloved, both animals
had to be housed, and the livery and the stable entered the
architectural scheme of things in the West.

67. Livery and stable, Pincher Station, Alberta.

68. Dog Creek, British Columbia.

69. Hornitos, California.

70. Nevada City, Montana.

71. Sheridan, Montana.

72. Bodie, California.

74. Cody, Wyoming.

75. Telluride, Colorado.

76. Stable, Caldwell, Montana (overleaf).

77. Ochre River, Manitoba.

Country Ingenuity...

The need to improvise was by no means exclusive to those who came first in the settlement of the North American West. From the time within living memory it has often been necessary to make do, to fashion for themselves what could not be easily purchased, from sharpening-wheels to door and gate latches.

78. Sterling, Montana.

80. 153-Mile House, British Columbia.

79. Horsefly, British Columbia.

81. Tolstoi, Manitoba.

Farm Graphics...

Find a wall and tell the folks what you've got to sell—
although these advertisements lack some of the splendiferous qualities of the barn billboards, they got the message
across and suggest that one of the earliest and most lucrative
trades a man could take up in the West was that of sign-
painting.

84. Carstairs, Alberta.

85. Burstall, Saskatchewan.

82. Cabri, Saskatchewan.

86. Carroll, Manitoba.

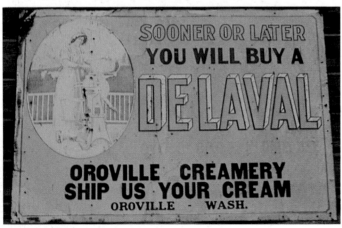

83. Molson, Washington.

87. Walsh, Alberta.

88. Armstrong, British Columbia.

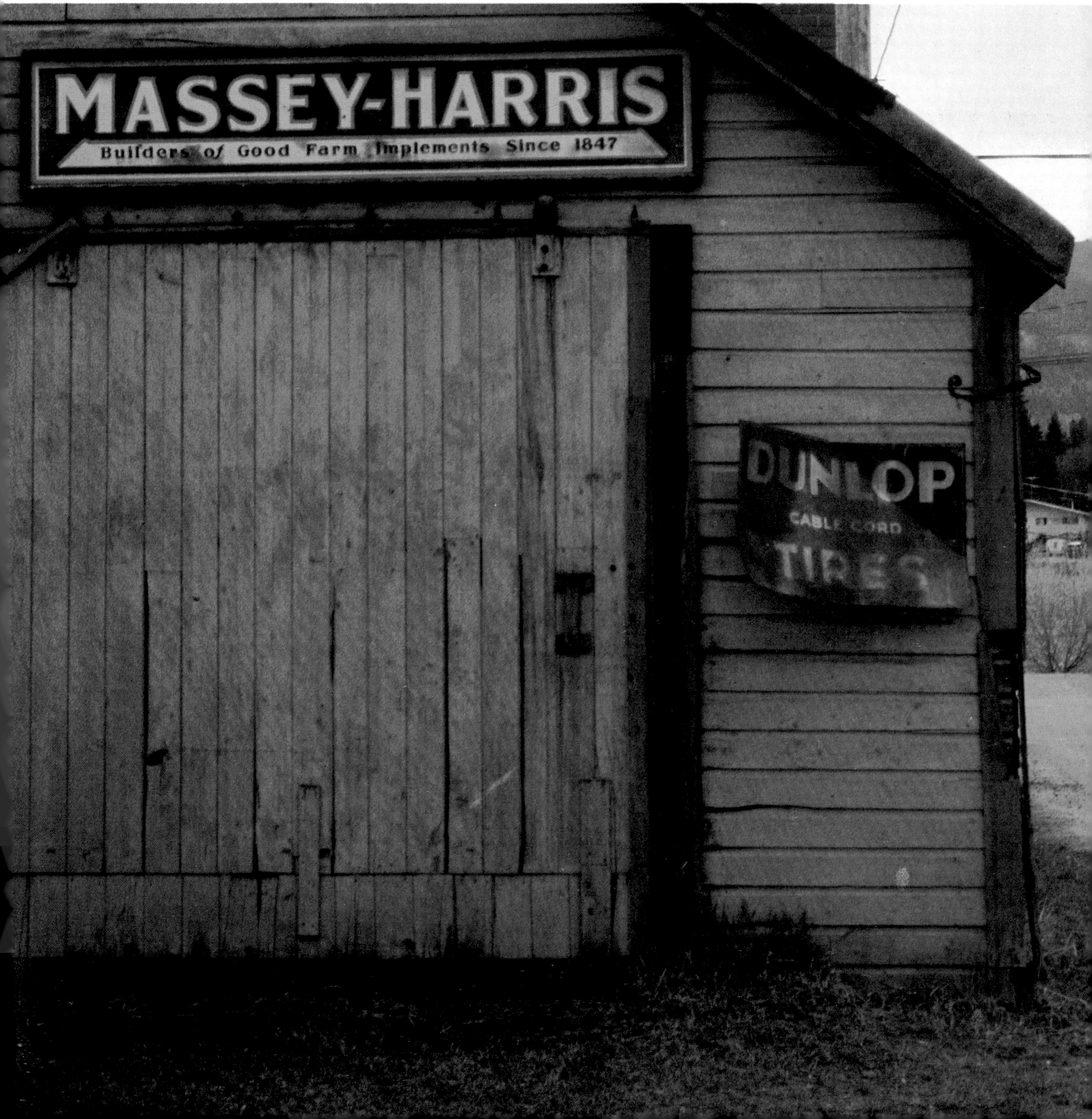

Some Native Stone...

As noted in the first chapter of this book, one built with what one could lay hands on. Stone, for obvious reasons of durability and strength, was much to be preferred when it could be obtained, and it was used now and then for some rather remarkable structures—such as the stone slaughterhouse in Shoshone, Idaho [91], which featured a wooden water tank for cleaning butchered meat. Even more remarkable is the rambling edifice, big enough to be called a mansion, near Manor, Saskatchewan [89]. It was built by the three Beckton brothers—Earnest, William, and Bertram—who

came from England in 1889 and set themselves up in style. Wealthy bachelors and erstwhile sportsmen, they built this stone house, as well as a 120-foot-long stone stable, bred race horses, imported fox hounds, started a hunt club, brought in bull terriers for badger-baiting, played rugby, cricket, and tennis, and threw splendid parties. By 1900, they had gone through most of their money and abandoned the country—and a little bit of England in the old West went with them.

90. Whitehall, Montana.

91. Shoshone, Idaho.

94. Two Guns, Arizona.

92. St. Onge, South Dakota.

93. Shingle Springs, California.

95. Harrisburg, Utah.

96. Lipton, Saskatchewan.

Until the advent of the internal-combustion engine, the farms of the West—or at least those large enough to afford them—heard the clatter and thump of steam tractors as they hauled plows, cultivators, and harvesting combines through the fields. The Case model shown [97] probably dates from about 1890. Also shown are the metal seat of another tractor of the period [99], a plow [98], and an old combine [100].

Huffers and Puffers...

98. Gascoigne, Manitoba.

99. Fort Steele, British Columbia.

100. Molson, Washington.

Silos and Granaries...

One of the most important functions on any working farm has always been the storage of winter feed for livestock, and —as always—the structures built for this purpose vary according to the tastes, skills, and financial wherewithal of the individual farmer. The intricately-contrived, though somewhat ramshackle crib [101], for example, doubtless was used to store corn for the utlimate fattening of hogs, while the ambitious pair of capped silos [104], roofed to protect against the heavy rains of the Fraser Valley, were built to hold silage—probably alfalfa—for the animals of a most substantial enterprise indeed.

101. Hardman, Oregon.

102. Wrentham, Alberta.

103. Almira, Washington.

104. Nicomen Island, British Columbia.

105. Waterville, Washington.

Skyscrapers of the Plains...

The high plains, spreading for thousands of square miles over much of Wyoming, Montana, western Manitoba, and Saskatchewan, have one inescapable feature—a sheer flatness only occasionally interrupted by low, rolling swells much like those of an ocean on a very calm day. Indeed, the land has more than once been described as "a sea of grass," and to stand in it, trapped beneath the great blue bowl of the

106. Norris, Montana.

sky, looking at the four horizons stretching out until lost in the mists of distance, is to acquire a new understanding of the term, "open space." In such a setting the great grain elevators that have punctuated the landscape at various railheads since the nineteenth century possess a structural impact that rivals that of any urban skyscraper. Visible for miles before you come to them, those that are left stand as comforting reminders of civilization in a land that too often seems bent on overwhelming man's petty ambitions for himself.

107. Balcarres, Saskatchewan.

108. Spillimacheen, British Columbia (overleaf).

Water Towers...

In spite of its appearance, the large structure [115] is not the remains of a frontier fort—it is a water tower, larger than most, but serving precisely the same function as the smaller creations shown. It was the "waterworks" for the town of Shaniko, Oregon—once, by its own lights, the "wool-shipping center of the world," but now almost completely abandoned—and the purpose it served was quite as necessary as protection from Indians: the storage and distribution of water, the single most precious commodity in the frontier West.

110. Mendocino, California.

111. Blue Lake, California.

115. Shaniko, Oregon.

109. Fairfield, California.

112. Ridgefield, Washington.

113. Sheridan, Wyoming.

114. Douglas City, California.

The Canadian Ukraine...

Of all the immigrant stocks that entered the Canadian West —and they were quite as astonishingly diverse as those of the western United States—one of the most recent and largest has been the Ukrainian. Fleeing the turmoil and uncertainty of the years just before, during, and after the Russian Revolution, Ukrainians in Canada increased from fewer than twenty-five thousand in 1900 to more than one hundred thousand by 1920. Most were farmers, and they moved naturally into that part of Canada that reminded them of the landscape of their homeland—the high plains and central lowlands of Manitoba, Saskatchewan, and Alberta. With them, as these photographs show, they brought their old world concepts of rural architecture, and their farmhouses, barns, and villages provided a splendid touch of the exotic to the new land.

116. Henrietta, Saskatchewan.

117. Thrums, British Columbia.

120. Calder, Saskatchewan.

118. Calder, Saskatchewan.

119. MacNutt, Saskatchewan.

The Last Thatch Roof...

121. Caliento, Manitoba.

122. Caliento, Manitoba.

123. Caliento, Manitoba.

In Caliento, Manitoba, stands one of the most curious and quietly moving of all the relics recorded in this book—a tiny, thatch-roofed cottage that is surely one of the last, if not **the** last, of its kind. It was built in 1911 by a Ukrainian farmer and has housed three families since. The latest owners, also Ukrainian, lived here from 1934 to 1967, and in this little house, barely larger than a suburban living room, heated during the long Manitoba winters by a pit dug in the floor for a fire, they raised five daughters to maturity.

Country Debris...

The detritus of a million lives. . . . In 1890, the United States Bureau of the Census declared that the frontier had closed, been filled in, been conquered. No such announcement came from Canadian authorities, and those still attempting to fill in and conquer the plains west of Winnipeg and north all the way to the Peace River might have given that conclusion some argument; so might have those who struggled into the Yukon in the last of the great gold rushes in 1897 and 1898. Still, these were but frontier pockets, the last expressions of the westward movement, one of the great events of human history. To commemorate the passage of that movement we have built monuments of stone and concrete, contrived statues, laid down plaques and markers. But the people who made that movement left behind their own kind of monuments—buckboards and teamsters' wagons, wagon wheels and sewing machines, bits and pieces of lives that come down to us only as distant memories.

124. Sandon, British Columbia.

125. Trailtown Village, Cody, Wyoming.

126. Bodie, California.

130. Virginia City, Montana.

127. Antelope, Oregon.

131. Dog Creek Indian Reserve, British Columbia.

128. Calico, California.   129. Shaniko, Oregon.

132. Cody, Wyoming.   133. Fort Steele, British Columbia.

134. Douglas, Washington (overleaf).

The Towns

"I only wish that the vulgar,
snobbish custom of attaching
'City' to every place of
more than three houses could
be stopped...."

Boosterism has by no means been a phenomenon peculiar to the North American West. Yet there has rarely been anything sedate about the history of the West; if it has sometimes been a theatre of the absurd, it has never been one of pinchpenny visions. In this arena of large excitements and ostensibly limitless potential, boosterism has flourished like a hothouse flower, and it has only been in recent years that we have come to learn, sometimes painfully, that growth is not necessarily progress, that much of what it brings has come at the expense of values which in the long run may have been far more important to our civilization.

To those who first came to this land, of course, such an idea would have been anathema. If they had paid any attention to it whatever, they would have dismissed it as the demented product of a certifiable lunatic. They were unsullied by doubt. They were **builders**, beGod, and what they built were cities — or at least towns which at one time or another in their careers were considered to have reasonable expectations of becoming cities. Of all the outsized developments the West has witnessed, perhaps none was so astounding as the number of towns spawned from about 1850 to the turn of the century. There were, quite literally, thousands scattered from Juneau, Alaska, to Shakespeare, New Mexico, many of which did not vanish and some of which ultimately put the lie to Bayard Taylor's complaint of 1866: ''I only wish that the vulgar, snobbish custom of attaching 'City' to every place of more than three houses could be stopped.'' What is more, with the exception of those that had started on the foundation of settlements established by the Spanish in earlier centuries, each of these thousands of settlements was conjured into existence, invented, frequently at dizzying speed.

In the spring of 1879, for example, the mining camp of Leadville, Colorado, was just suffering the pangs of boom and could be described by Helen Hunt Jackson as ''all log cabins, or else plain, unpainted board shanties. Some of the cabins seem to burrow in the ground; others are set up on posts, like roofed bedsteads. Tents, wigwams of bare poles, with a blackened spot in front, where somebody slept last night, but will never sleep in again; cabins wedged in between stumps, cabins built on stumps, cabins with chimneys made of flower-pots or bits of stove pipe...cabins half roofed; cabins with sail-cloth roofs; cabins with no roof at all—this represents the architecture of Leadville homes." Three years later, its mines prospering and eastern and foreign investment coming in hand-over-fist, Leadville had become so well-established a city that it brought nothing but disgust from a visiting Englishman: "Leadville was like some provincial town. The men would not have looked out of place in the street, say, of Reading, while the women in their quiet and somewhat old-fashioned style of dressing reminded me very curiously of rural England. Indeed, I do not think my anticipations have ever been so completely upset as in Leadville."

Guthrie, Oklahoma Territory, provides an even more remarkable instance of growth. In April 1889, although officially laid out, the "town" consisted of one tiny depot, one Wells Fargo Office, and one twenty by forty foot land office—all of it waiting for some fifteen thousand land-hungry "sooners" to burst into sight when the government opened the region to settlement [it had been Indian Territory since the 1830s]. That came on April 22. By April 27, it was a tent city; by the middle of May a makeshift metropolis complete with restaurants, barber shops, merchandise stores, a post office, a two-story hotel, and fifty saloons; and by September, a fitting site for Oklahoma's first territorial capital, possessing a stable population of nearly twenty thousand, a Westinghouse electric light plant, city parks, a chartered streetcar line, a public waterworks system, and the all-brick Commercial Banking Company building, the most impressive structure in several thousand square miles.

Not all towns grew so quickly or achieved such permanence as Leadville and Guthrie, but nearly all followed a pattern of evolution that was similar. Most were speculations based on boom or the expectation of boom. A far-sighted speculator or group of speculators would keep an eye on developing possibilities [mining, land, timber, a coming railroad] and when the time seemed ripe invest not in the products themselves but in town lots, sometimes even platting out the very town. By this simple expedient, such men would quickly find themselves at the top of a little urban heap: those wishing to provide goods and services to the individuals who were out in the field digging for gold or farming or cutting down trees were dependent on the speculators for the lots on which to build their businesses; the bigger the boom, the more valuable the lots and the more expensive rentals and sales became. Quite often, of course, merchants and speculators were one and the same; quite often, they miscalculated the lasting power of any given boom and were ruined; quite often, enormous frauds were perpetrated. But for those who guessed right, the rewards were high indeed. In 1872, for example, a pair of liquor dealers determined the right-of-way of the then-building Santa Fe Railroad, picked out a site just west of Fort Dodge, Kansas, and set up shop. Others drifted in, and by the middle of July a corporation was formed and the town of Dodge City platted. Very soon, it was the major shipping center for a flourishing trade in buffalo hides and when that died down was more than ready to become one of the principle cattle-shipping towns during the boom years of the 1870s and early 1880s.

Except for the tiny farming communities sprinkled here and there throughout the West, which were built less on the concept of boom than on that of a slow, steady, long-term growth, most towns displayed a common social development. Whether a mining town, a cattle town, or a railroad head, each went through a period of what can only be described as frenzy. Speculators, lawyers, real estate brokers, merchants, gamblers, saloonkeepers, newspapermen, laborers, and crooks attended the first labor pains of the town's birth, milling about in the muddy or dusty streets, chattering in a constant hum, buying, selling, drinking, carousing, keeping an eye on the main chance. Around and over it all was the sound of birth: the clattering of wagons bringing in lumber, tools, beer, liquor, and foodstuffs, the inspired profanity of teamsters, the sounds of hammers and saws. Within days, the raw outlines of the town would be up; tents would have been replaced by falsefronts and the streets more clearly defined and sometimes lined with wooden sidewalks; by then, the prostitutes would have arrived, slightly softening the raw edges of life. Infancy would have been attained, but the town was still far removed from, say, the Guthrie, Oklahoma, of September 1889. It would more likely share the qualities of Deadwood, South Dakota, as described by a newspaper reporter in 1877: "Deadwood is a city of a single street, and a most singular street it is. The buildings which grace its sides are a curiosity in modern architecture, and their light construction is a standing insult to every wind that blows. Paint is a luxury only indulged in by the aristocracy. . . . Wells are dug in the middle of the street, all sorts of building material occupies them and every manner of filth is thrown into them. . . ."

It was at such a stage that such towns gave birth to all the legends that we have bundled up into the general term, the "wild west." Boiling with humanity, most of it young men full of the juices of life, there was in these towns more than a little random violence. Writing in his diary, George Whitwell Parsons reported on his first day in Tombstone, Arizona, in 1880: "Shooting this a.m. and two fellows in afternoon attempted to go for one another with guns and six-shooters—but friends interposed. . . . Talk of killing indulged in again tonight. Everyone goes heeled." That Tombstone was markedly more dangerous a town than, for example, Des Moines, Iowa, in 1880 can hardly be argued; yet it may have been the exception rather than the rule among western towns. Even Deadwood—where Wild Bill Hickok died over the dead man's hand and Deadwood Dick and Calamity Jane performed their didoes—could be declared almost bucolic by the newspaper reporter of 1877: "A keen-eyed, money-grubbing set of men makes up the population, but they are far from the bloodthirsty scoundrels the average newspaper correspondent makes them out to be. Shooting is not frequent; fighting is only occasional; and property is perfectly secure." Mining engineer Henry Janin agreed the following year: "It is...one of the pleasantest of all mining localities I have visited; and in no other district is justice more ably administered, or greater security afforded to life and property." Even Dodge City, which enjoyed styling itself "The Wickedest Little City in America," a characterization certainly capitalized on by a century's-worth of cheap entertainment, may not have deserved its reputation. In **The Cattle Towns**, historian Robert R. Dykstra calculated that between the years 1870 and 1885, the boom years of the cattle trade, the cow towns of Abilene, Ellsworth, Wichita, Dodge City, and Caldwell could only put together among them forty-five genuine homicides—and Dodge City, the grand champion of them all, had only fifteen, a murder rate comparable to many a medium-sized town today.

However justified the western town's reputation for violence may have been, the phase which produced it was consistently brief. Towns which for all their spontaneous creation and color were in fact economic centers needed and actively pursued stability, particularly if the booms which had given them birth had any lasting power. Business, generally speaking, abhors chaos and will not tolerate anarchy. When there was money to be made, the rugged individualist who thumbed his nose at stability was liable to find himself hanging from the long end of a short rope, as the criminal element of San Francisco learned during the vigilante actions of 1851 and 1856, and as the members of the notorious Plummer gang learned during similar activities in Montana in 1864.

If the transition between the frenzy of birth and the somewhat more controlled frenetic activity of adolescence was brief, so too was that between adolescence and maturity. While many western towns did—and do—attempt to retain some of the more lurid attractiveness of their pasts, the fact is that most became very much like their counterparts in the east. Civic improvement was the order of the day, and probably nothing more solidly established the difference between legend and reality, for it indicates the fact that residents had acquired a stake in the area; they intended to stay, perhaps even to rear families around them in the finest pioneer tradition, and were willing to sacrifice at least part of the quick dollar in exchange for a livable environment. Cobblestoned and Macadamized streets, gas and electricity systems, sewer systems, water lines, and public transportation were among the refinements visible in various towns as early as the middle 1880s —in regions that little more than a generation before had been as unfamiliar with civilized trappings as the mountains of the moon. Business sections, where applicable, took on the massive solidity of brick or stone architecture, and homes acquired lawns and gardens. Fire departments—at first voluntary and later municipally owned and operated—were organized and equipment purchased. They were never enough for a great many towns, but they were an earnest attempt to control the single worst problem the western town had to deal with.

Towns acquired one or more major hotels, some of them to challenge the best the east had to offer—the Brown Palace in Denver, the Palace in San Francisco, the International in Virignia City, Nevada, and the Clarendon in Cripple Creek were prime examples. Schools and churches, social clubs and reading societies attended themselves to the higher needs of the mind and soul, while music halls, theatres, and opera houses [few of them having anything to do with opera] satisfied the craving for more rambunctious entertainment. The opera house, in fact, was a particularly symbolic manifestation of civic arrival; the town that could afford a theatre of such a size and architecture to be called an opera house was a town to be reckoned with.

Add to such things the fact that nearly every sizable town in the West had some sort of railroad and telegraph connection with the centers of the east by the turn of the century, and it is clear that applying the word "frontier" to such muscular exercises in municipal growth is not only inaccurate but also misleading. To go further and assume that the peculiarly undisciplined, free-wheeling life of the early western towns was translated whole into a metropolitan structure is to write history as we like it, not as it was. Boosterism had won.

Main Street...

Before it was sold to a real estate developer, Lot No. 3 of the Metro-Goldwyn-Mayer studios in Hollywood featured a painstaking reproduction of the main street of a typical American western town—complete with a saloon, a bank, a livery stable, a restaurant, an hotel, a stage office, a blacksmith shop, a feed store, a general store, a barber shop, a dress shop, a sheriff's office, a jail, wooden sidewalks, and a dusty street down which a couple of gunslingers could walk for the inevitable showdown. It had everything, in fact, except a bordello, since in those days Hollywood could not bring itself to admit that the typical western town contained such a thing; today, undoubtedly, something would be provided. In any case, this ersatz little town—together with its counterparts in other Hollywood studios—depicted in hundreds of movies seen by millions of people over more than two generations, became the living image of what most of us came to think the western town of history looked like. As these photographs demonstrate, however, unlike most things learned from the movies, this image was remarkably authentic.

137. Moorcroft, Wyoming.

138. Saco, Montana.

135. Ranfurly, Alberta.

136. Victor, Colorado.

139. Calder, Saskatchewan.

140. Walnut Grove, California.

141. Shackleton, Saskatchewan.

143. Sundance, Wyoming.

142. Borden, Saskatchewan.

144. Eatonia, Saskatchewan.

145. Fairplay, Colorado.

147. Silver City, Idaho.

152. Hardman, Oregon (overleaf).

150. Genoa, Nevada.

151. Wolf Point, Montana.

146. Wetaskiwin, Alberta.

148. Ouray, Colorado.

149. Silver Plume, Colorado.

153. Tulameen, British Columbia.

157. Locke, California.

154. Cymric, Saskatchewan.

158. Chitwood, Oregon.

155. Bear Valley, California.   156. Yampa, Colorado.

159. Keystone, South Dakota.   160. Grassy Lake, Alberta.

The Old-Time General Store...

For generations, the country store was the center of its own small universe. Here was everything that personified civilized life in the essentially rural regions of the North American West. Not merely goods—the flour and lard and sugar and coffee, the utensils and tools and harnesses, the calico and gingham, ribbons, buttons, and braids, drugs and patent medicines, kerosene and gun oil, ax helves and two-bladed Barlow knives, rock candy, horehound, and lemon drops, ten for a penny—but even the reassuring forms of society. Most general stores also doubled as the local post office; the owner quite often served as the justice of the peace or as town clerk and notary public, and virtually every bit of business, public or private, could be taken care of here in one Saturday trip once a month or once every two months.

161. Athalmer, British Columbia.

162. Sutter Creek, California.

Country Graphics...

One of the saddest things about our new society as it busily tears things down in order to build things up is that we lose so many details along the way, interruptions and curiosities that delight the eye and engage the imagination. Concrete, glass, and plastic are doubtless admirable building materials, but is there anything about them that would make us want to reach out and touch them, as we would a brick wall with its Coca-Cola sign, or inspire us to watch what they do, as we would a weather vane turning with the vagaries of the wind?

163. Hardman, Oregon.

164. Saskatoon, Saskatchewan.

165. Edgely, Saskatchewan.

166. Jerome, Arizona.

167. Moorcroft, Wyoming.

168. Hilton, California.

Gas Stations and Petrol Pumps...

For anyone born in the years just before World War I, perhaps the most compelling touchstone of nostalgia is a remembrance of what may legitimately be called the golden age of the automobile—an era of revolutionary convenience and mobility that was touched with the unmistakable aroma of adventure. The age did not start out that way, of course; an early Vermont law, for example, required that any automobile in operation be preceded by a "responsible adult" waving a red flag, and in the United States President Woodrow Wilson once warned that: "Nothing has spread socialistic feeling in this country more than the use of the automobile. To the countryman, they are a picture of the arrogance of wealth, with all its independence and carelessness." Wilson misread the temper of the times and most assuredly misread the "countryman," who within a few years of first exposure seized upon the automobile and made it his own. No more the big Studebaker wagon for Saturday trips to town—now it was more than likely one of Henry Ford's "tin lizzies," which gasped, snorted, rattled, and backfired, but got to town nevertheless, and could travel farther and faster than anything the farmer or rancher had ever known. Soon, every hamlet of distinction from Alexandria, British Columbia, to Goldfield, Nevada, had its contingent of Ford dealerships, garages, and service stations with their elegant pumps that vaguely resembled street lamps from the Victorian Age. Most of these artifacts—like many of the towns in which they stood—are gone, now, replaced by the neon clusters of service stations that line freeways, thruways, and parkways, the modern ganglia of the North American West.

170. Medicine Hat, Alberta.

169. Brock, Saskatchewan.

171. Chilcotin Plateau, British Columbia (overleaf).

172. Spearfish, South Dakota.

173. Spring Coulée, Alberta.

174. Goldfield, Nevada.

175. Frenchtown, Montana.

176. Granum, Alberta.

177. Ruff, Washington.

180. Westbourne, Manitoba.

178. Tarkio, Montana.

179. Wardner, British Columbia.

181. Alexandria, British Columbia.

183. Yahk, British Columbia.

184. Slocan, British Columbia.

185. Madison, Saskatchewan.

182. Bodie, California.

The Auto Graveyard...

One of the more popular songs of the automobile's golden age was "The Auto's the Pleasure for Me," and it rattled along at a lively Model-T pace: "You may sing of life's many pleasures,/ Of whatever they may be,/ Of boating and bathing and baseball,/ But the auto's the one for me./ For as it runs along smoothly,/ Without a jolt or jar,/ One might think that they were riding/ In a Pullman Palace car." Alas, neither the song nor the kind of automobile it sang about survived the era. In the West, far removed from industrial centers where they might be sold for scrap, the problem arose of what to do with an automobile that had seen its last days. The solution was simple and pragmatic: leave it where it died. The practice continues, obviously, for one cannot approach or leave a town of nearly any size in the far West without encountering grubby little pockets of abandoned automobiles on the outskirts, rusting toward eternity. It is not the most endearing of western traditions.

186. Barkerville, British Columbia.

188. Bindloss, Alberta.

187. Bodie, California.

189. Langham, Saskatchewan.

The Village Barbershop...

It has frequently been observed that the North American West as a civilization was almost entirely masculine, at least during most of the nineteenth century. Oh, women were **there**, of course—as sweethearts, wives, mothers, "schoolmarms," or prostitutes, embodying a gentleness that softened all the hard edges of wilderness—but it was men who plowed the land, raised the cattle, mined the treasure, and made all the important political, social, and economic decisions. Perhaps. One is inclined to wonder, however, why it was that men found it necessary to retreat so often to such masculine institutions as the saloon, the lodgehall, and even the barbershop, where they could be lathered from their private shaving mugs, exchange earthy observations, and peruse the latest editions of the **National Police Gazette** or **Captain Billy's Whiz-Bang**. Might it be that these horny-handed sons of toil and rugged individualists were escaping an influence they could not admit?

192. Paradise Valley, Alberta.

193. Strasbourg, Saskatchewan.

191. Silverton, Colorado.

194. Ashcroft, British Columbia.

196. Goldfield, Colorado.

197. Central City, South Dakota.

195. Nevada City, California.

198. Moyie, British Columbia.

200. Park City, Utah.

Firehalls...

One of the clearest and most consistently present dangers of any western town was the threat of fire, since most were constructed almost entirely of wood. Consequently, just about the first thing responsible town fathers put into effect was to organize a volunteer fire department, build a fire hall, and—if the funds could be raised—buy a fire engine, whether a hand pumper or a horse-drawn steam pumper with plenty of shining brass. Not that it always did much good. Among the western towns that burned down at least once in their careers were Virginia City, Nevada; Nome, Alaska; Bisbee, Arizona; Tombstone, Arizona; Cripple Creek, Colorado; Wallace, Idaho; Helena, Montana; and San Francisco, California, which was destroyed no fewer than six times between 1849 and 1851.

199. Columbia, California.

201. Barkerville, British Columbia.

The Blacksmith...

Even to be considered a proper town, the typical western hamlet had to include at least one of the following: a saloonkeeper, a lawyer, a banker, an hotelkeeper, a storekeeper, a newspaper editor, a barber, and a blacksmith. That was the minimum, and of them all the most indispensable was the blacksmith, for it was this swarthy, sweating Vulcan of the West, with his bellows, his anvil, and his fire, who kept things going—shoeing horses and mules, forging wheelrims, hinges, hooks, nails, horseshoes, latches, and, in later years, making replacement parts for tractors, trucks, and automobiles. A man of parts—most of them made by himself.

203. Silverton, Colorado.

206. Blairmore, Alberta.

204. Claresholm, Alberta.

205. Armstrong, British Columbia.

207. Gooding, Idaho.

208. Didsbury, Alberta.

209. Silver City, Idaho (overleaf).

213. Ouray, Colorado.

210. Georgetown, California.

214. Deadwood, South Dakota.

211. Jerome, Arizona.

212. Ymir, British Columbia.

215. Jacksonville, Oregon.

216. Georgetown, Colorado.

The Hotels...

Most western towns possessed one sort of hotel or another — sometimes little more than a couple of rooms with ratty cots available for two bits a night — but the biggest, the best, and the most fancy establishments were found almost exclusively in mining towns. The reason was simple enough: by their very nature, mining towns attracted swarms of transients, some of them miners but most of them folks who were more interested in picking clean the miner than picking treasure out of the earth — and most had money to spend. So it was that the great hostelries of the West could offer brass beds and downy pillows, indoor plumbing (sometimes right in the room itself), a mirrored mahogany bar, and a restaurant quite capable of serving up with regularity such esoteric items as terrapin soup, eastern oysters, or trout, all of it washed down with the finest of French wines and champagnes.

217. French Gulch, California.

218. Tulameen, British Columbia.

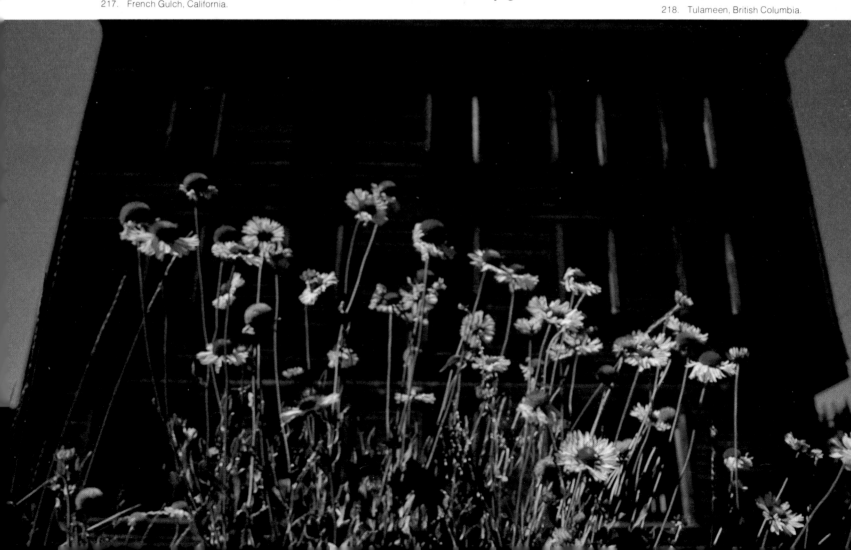

The Brewery...

Beer, that sparkling, golden refresher, has been kicking
around in human affairs longer than anyone knows. What
we do know is that it has been a popular drink at least since
the great age of Mesopotamia seven thousand years before
the birth of Christ, that it became an item of daily consump-
tion in Babylonia, that it was so widespread in ancient Egypt
that the government put a tax on it, that the Romans were
not unacquainted with it as they invaded the continent of
Europe, that it ultimately spread from Spain to England, and
from thence to the New World and finally across the rivers
and mountains into the North American West. Beer was as
common as blowflies in the West, if considerably more wel-
come. Most of it was imported in great wooden kegs from
the established brewing centers of the East, but here and
there an enterprising individual put together his own town
brewery. And why not? What better oil was available to
lubricate the wheels of civilization?

221. Fairplay (South Park City), Colorado.

220. Virginia City, Montana.

The Houses of Town...

Shortly after the turn of the century, the greatest of all western historians, Hubert Howe Bancroft, offered some trenchant observations on the role of the city in the shaping of the human condition. "In this day of great wealth and wonderful inventions," he wrote, "we realize more and more the value of the city to mankind. . . . Cities are not merely marts of commerce; they stand for civility; they are civilization itself. The city street is the school of philosophy, of art, of letters; city society is the home of refinement. In their reciprocal relations the city is as men make it, while from the citizen one may determine the quality of the city. The atmosphere of the city is an eternal force." Bancroft was writing in 1906 amid the ruins of a San Francisco—the definitive western boom town—that had been shaken and burned to the ground by the great earthquake and fire of that year, and there were only a handful of other towns in the West that might have inspired such lofty reflections: Denver, Colorado, perhaps; or Seattle, Washington; or even Helena, Montana; no more. Yet even in the smallest hamlet that breathed any kind of fire for the future, such sentiments would not have seemed out of place to those who had made their towns. That attitude is what these photographs illustrate, for these were not merely houses, they were **residences**. They were structures of substance—solid, spacious, even elegant, and they reflected almost precisely the psychological stance of those who had caused their construction. On however small a scale, the bankers, lawyers, and merchants who built such houses were striving for Bancroft's sense of **civitas**, that "eternal force" which would ensure permanence and prosperity and all that inevitably went with them, including philosophy, letters, arts, and refinement. They were wrong, as the present condition of the houses suggests; but the vision was not.

223. Silverton, Colorado.

224. Mendocino, California (overleaf).

225. Crested Butte, Colorado.

227. Ranchos de Taos, New Mexico.

226. Dillon, Montana.

228. Georgetown, Colorado.

229. Nevada City, Montana.

231. Bainville, Montana (overleaf).

232. Redcliff, Alberta.

233. Black Hawk, Colorado.

234. Coulterville, California.

235. Dayton, Nevada.

Lodge Halls...

For reasons best known to the muse of history—or the gremlin of tradition—one of the most persistent traits of western man has been the urge to band together into social organisms of no particular utilitarian value. It was true of the Romans; it was true of the pioneers who first thrust their way into what Lord James Bryce called the "silent, splendid Nature" of the Great West. Certainly there was reason enough in the demanding and sometimes hostile environment of the West for one to seek the company of others, some reassurance of not being alone in a land whose sky stretched to the horizon, and few western towns in the nineteenth century were without their meeting places for Masons, the Independent Order of Odd Fellows [I.O.O.F.], the International Order of Red Men [which had little or nothing to do with Indians], or the Woodmen of the World [which had nothing to do with lumbering]. They provided fellowship and occasional good works—and sometimes such splendid relics as the carved tower of the Masonic Hall [236].

237. Antelope, Oregon.

236. Mendocino, California.

238. Barkerville, British Columbia.

239. Index, Washington.

240. Jackson, Montana.

241. Jefferson Island, Montana (overleaf).

Turrets...

The later Victorian Age was a time of transition and change, a time when the full weight of the industrial revolution first fell upon all the institutions that had been so painstakingly developed over the preceding generations. Confusion was the consequence, and nowhere was it manifested more visibly than in the architecture of the era. Always inclined toward the eclectic, the Age embraced what was known as the "Queen Anne" style with a fevered enthusiasm, and in the process it tacked on towers and turrets to nearly every structure imaginable. The West was in no way immune to this curious inclination, and in its towns those who could afford it gave their homes and office buildings the vaguely brooding qualities of something that might have been seen in the English countryside eight hundred years ago. It was all supposed to add up to elegance, quality, and solid respectability —heavy-handed fairy castles for a western bourgeoisie.

244. Belle Fourche, South Dakota.

245. Wallace, Idaho.

242. Leadville, Colorado.

243. Dillon, Montana.

246. Rapid City, South Dakota.

247. Ellensburg, Washington.

248. Arcata, California.

Jailhouse Rock...

251. Yuma, Arizona.

In many of the towns of the West—particularly those of the mining and ranching frontiers—both the concept and the practice of law and order were generally freewheeling affairs, more a matter of expediency than of justice. To men in a hurry to make a pile and shake the dust of the town from their heels, "popular" [that is, vigilante] justice was quick, cheap, and it got the job done: you either flogged the offender, banished him, or, when it came down to it, hanged him—but you didn't worry about where you were going to put him. The attitude incurred the wrath of a contemporary social historian, Josiah Royce, who contemplated the mining camp experience in Gold Rush California in ironic terms: "Whose gold, now hoarded by the pound in insecure tents, the prey of every vagabond, might have contributed to build a strong jail . . . ? Or, perhaps, was it not of a truth felt unnecessary to build a strong jail—unnecessary just because one chose in one's heart, meanwhile, to think ropes a little cheaper than bricks, and, for the purpose, just as strong. . . ." In any town that outlasted the immediate greed of its founders, of course, society ultimately shook down into more respectable forms, and when such towns did get around to building jails, they tended to be sturdy, though not particularly aesthetic little structures, as the photographs shown here illustrate—especially that of Yuma Territorial Prison [251].

250. Hornitos, California.

252. Bannack, Montana.

253. Sheridan, Montana.

254. Twin Bridges, Montana.

The Schools and Churches

"…when we all sat down to our
elk meet, beens, coffee, and dryed
apples…these men who knew
little of law…who had not
prayed since they nelt at their
Mothers Knee bowed there heads
while you…gave thanks and
when you finished someone
said Amen."

Except for the true mavericks of the world, those misanthropists who trust only themselves, one of the strongest instincts of the human animal is the sense of community. We are a gregarious species—not merely because there is protection in numbers in a sometimes hostile environment, but also because the human intercourse which community provides nourishes the mind and heart; in others, we often find ourselves. Nowhere was this more true than in the West. Even when the sense of community was not formalized into an urban structure, it was still there, no matter in how deeply hidden a pocket of the mountains, no matter how far one tiny homestead shack might have been from another. It was important, when you were in fact alone, not to **feel** alone, and in such a context the visit to a neighbor or to the nearest hamlet, even if it took most or all of one or two days, was a necessary therapy, a reaching out for the assurance of community.

In large part, the glue that held the sense of community together was provided by the region's schools and churches. By the standards of the long-settled east, most of the representative examples of these two institutions in the West were primitive in the extreme. But they did the job that was required of them—often under the most adverse of circumstances.

Until well after the turn of the century—and in many parts of the region even longer than that—the western rural school was the very picture of crudity, both in appearance and performance. Local school districts were normally given the flimsiest of budgets with which to work, not out of any outrageous niggardliness, but because the communities that financed them had so little to spend on anything. As a result, the typical rural school was literally a one-room affair perched in the open at whatever point seemed most central to the farms that surrounded it. The best schools were narrow frame shacks with wooden floors, peaked roofs, bell towers, and sometimes bells; the worst were log cabins with packed-earth or clay floors. The best schools contained real desks and genuine blackboards; the worst contained rude, unfinished benches and boards that had been **painted** black. The best schools had an adequate supply of McGuffy's readers, Ray's arithmetic, the Eclectic history and geography, Webster's "blue-black speller," and Harvey's grammar; the worst might be able to lay hands on one or two of these, but not enough for all the pupils.

Rarely more than twenty pupils appeared at school at any one time, and the terms were adjusted to coincide with those periods of the year when the children were not needed at home or on the farm. For children too young to be of any practical use, there would be a few weeks of schooling in the summer. The rest, when the changeable weather permitted, attended during the winter, sometimes for no more than six weeks, sometimes for as much as three months. They ranged in age over a broad spectrum; in a single classroom there might be five-and-six-year-olds painfully studying their first McGuffy reader next to a twenty-year-old studying—often with equal pain—his last. There were no grades to speak of; each student moved ahead in his study as his own abilities dictated or the teacher determined. Scholastic standards were not high.

Nor were standards high for the teachers themselves. Given the salaries available and the consequent lack of men or women eager to get into the profession, a school district was more often than not willing to hire anyone who could demonstrate at least a marginal knowledge of the three Rs. Salaries ranged anywhere from twenty-five to thirty-five dollars a month and amounted to a good deal less than that simply because the terms were so short. Whether a man or a woman, one of the basic requirements of the job —one that sometimes exceeded in importance any teaching skills—was the ability to inflict discipline. In Barry Broadfoot's **The Pioneer Years**, a former "school-marm" outlined the problem: "Oh, they told me not to take that school. They said, 'You'll be eaten alive.' I guess they were right because that school had already run out two teachers in the past two years.... It was the big boys that was doing it.... People think children today can be bad. They were bad then. Bad. If their dad couldn't lick them on the farm, they'd lick him and then they'd beat up on the teacher. Believe me, it happened....

"The first day in school I looked the class over and I knew I had to be fierce. They wouldn't get me, no sirree. That first morning I went into the drawer and I got out the big leather strap and I took a good fierce grip on it. I said I wonder what we have here and I held it up and then I smacked it down as hard as I could on my desk. Then I smacked it down hard again and again. I was showing them I could hit." After applying that persuasive strap on one recalcitrant young man "bigger than me, mind you," and wearing the same glowering mask of imminent threat, things got better: "After about a month I did let up on them.... The little children got that scared look off their faces and were learning and the big boys, they started helping out and learning too.... Then I'd smile a bit."

Understandably, the quality of education that blossomed in such unpromising surroundings was several cuts below brilliance, if several cuts above outright ignorance. Henry Seidel Canby summed it up succinctly in **The Age of Confidence**: "We got discipline of the kind that teaches to do it now and don't ask foolish questions.... We got reading and reciting; and for the rest of the time were inflated with the rapidly multiplying volume of things to know which was to leave most of us with cluttered minds and weakened judgment." And yet, almost in spite of itself, the western rural school system once in a while did strike fire in some child. One such was Hamlin Garland, who in later years paid tribute to the McGuffy's readers he had encountered in his own one-room school. They were, he said, "almost the only counter-checks to the current of vulgarity and baseness which ran through the talk of the older boys, and I wish to acknowledge my deep obligation to Professor McGuffy, whoever he may have been, for the dignity and literary grace of his selections...."

A little learning may or may not be a dangerous thing, but for most of the children of the West it was all they got. For some, it was enough; for others, only the beginning.

Religion, of course, has had a longer history in the West than education, and in many respects has played a much larger role in its development. In the beginning, in fact, religion went hand-in-hand with empire-building. The Spanish, moving up from Mexico in the sixteenth century, brought priests with them whose duty it was to harvest souls among the heathen Indians and thereby assure not only an available supply of labor but also provide for the stability which settlement required. By the end of the eighteenth century, the Spanish mission system had spread in little frontier pockets through southern Mexico and Arizona and up the coast of California from San Diego to San Francisco. When Spain's thrust north succumbed to depleting wars on the European continent and growing pressures from an expanding American population, she withdrew from the country she had tamed—but the religion which had helped to tame it remained, providing islands of stability around which future growth could develop.

The northwest got its own taste of missionary settlement in the 1830s. In 1836, Marcus Whitman, with his wife, one other couple, and two single men, journeyed from St. Louis to Oregon as Methodist missionaries. Two missions were established, one at Waiilatpu, the other at Lapwai, and over the next eleven years struggled toward permanence, hampered both by Indian hostility and Whitman's narrow view of native customs and his impatience in getting them to accept the word of God as Whitman interpreted it. In 1847, during a measles epidemic which the Indians blamed on him, Whitman, his wife, and twelve other people were massacred, and the Methodist missionary movement in Oregon nearly came to a stop. Other missions were more fortunate—and more successful. In 1838, the Bishop of Quebec appointed Abbé Francois Norbet Blanchet as Vicar General of Oregon with Abbé Modeste Demers as his assistant, and the two had soon established a mission at Cowlitz to deal with the Indians; as well, they provided irregular services to the handful of French-Canadian settlers in the Willamette Valley. They were soon in gentle competition with Father Pierre De Smet, who was sent to Oregon by the St. Louis Jesuit novitiate in 1840 and, after establishing his first mission of St. Mary's in the Bitteroot Valley, went on to build six more throughout much of the territory's interior. More tolerant of the ways of the Indians and extremely patient in their teaching of the word, the Catholic missions prospered.

By far the most remarkable of all the religious exercises in the early years in the West were those of the Church of Jesus Christ of Latter-day Saints—the Mormons. They came not to convert, but to escape and to build. Born of the visions of Joseph Smith in 1836, possessed of a certain arrogance common to all sects who are convinced that they and they alone have found the True Path, vigorous and competitive businessmen, and devout practitioners of polygamy, the Mormons had more than a little difficulty in getting along with their neighbors. After years of bickering and sometimes violent persecution—climaxed when their founder was murdered in Nauvoo, Illinois—Smith's successor, Brigham Young, determined to take his people deep into the West, where they could follow their dream unmolested. The new Zion was Utah, deep in the heart of the Great Basin, and its headquarters was Salt Lake City, founded in 1846 near the shores of the great lake from which it took its name. Over the next thirty years, until Young's own death in 1877, the Mormons entrenched themselves in the entire Great Basin, built cities and towns, successfully proselytized for converts all over the world, and developed the largest and most successful theocracy in the history of this continent.

For most of the western pioneers, however, religion was apt to be a good deal more slapdash and disorganized an affair than either the Spanish, the early missionary, or the Mormon experiences. Except for the roughest of the mining camps, which characteristically had no sense of community and whose denizens saw no immediate need of religious solace, this was not for lack of piety; it was for lack of money. While most communities could afford to pool labor and resources for the construction of some kind of church, few could afford the services of a full-time minister, of whatever persuasion. So administering the word of God was largely in the hands of the circuit-rider, the wandering religious minstrel who traveled a long circuit from town to town, bringing the people Sunday services on an irregular basis.

He also brought the summer camp meeting, a days-long ritual which not only refurbished the faith of those who might have backslid, brought forth new witnesses for Christ, and provided for the rites of baptism, but also gave folks for miles around the opportunity to abandon chores with a clear conscience and gather with people they had not seen for months, the adults to exchange gossip and field talk, the younger children to throw themselves wildly into group games and fights, the older children to begin the complicated and mysterious business of courtship, without which there would have **been** no civilization in the West. It was a lively and satisfying time, camp-meeting week, and when it was done the people returned to responsibility much enlarged in spirit—not just because of the reacquaintance with the trappings of formal religion, but also because they had, one more time, enjoyed the reassurance of human contact.

Until well after the turn of the century, the circuit-rider, or "Sam Singer" [for Psalm Singer], remained the principal religious agent over much of the West, furiously dedicated, as persevering as any hardscrabble farmer in the practice of his trade, remarkably durable in the demanding task of bringing the word to everyone he could reach. Perhaps the most remarkable of them all was the Reverend Wesley Van Orsdel. He came to the Blackfoot reservation of Montana in 1872 to work with the Indians who promptly dubbed him "Great Heart," but after a year came to the conclusion that his own people had greater need of him. He forthwith took to the circuit, one which encompassed nearly all of Montana, and over the next forty years became quite possibly the single most influential religious man in the territory, eventually establishing more than one hundred Methodist churches. Called "Brother Van" by one and all, he captured not only souls, but also hearts—and this included the most elusive of them all, the cowboy, whose religious convictions commonly matched the sentiments once expressed by old Jesse Chisholm: "I do not know anything about the Bible. I have no use for preachers. No man ever came to me hungry and went away unfed, or naked and departed unclad. All my life I have tried to live at peace with my fellow man and be a brother to him. The rest I leave with the Great Spirit who placed me here, and whom I trust to do all things well."

But "Brother Van" was no ordinary preacher, and his effectiveness was documented forever by the western artist Charles M. Russell. In a letter sent to Van Orsdel near the end of his ministry in 1918, Russell recalled in his splendid orthography the first of their many encounters: "I was the only stranger to you so after Bab interduced Kid Russell he took me to one side and whispered.

"Boy, says he, I dont savy many samsingers but Bro. Van deals square and when we all sat down to our elk meet, beens, coffee and dryed apples under the rays of a bacon grease light, these men who knew little of law and one among them wore notches on his gun, men who had not prayed since they nelt at their Mothers Knee bowed there heads while you Bro Van gave thanks and when you finished someone said Amen. I am not sure but I think it was a man who I heard later was ore had been a rode agent.'"Russell concludes his letter with a sentiment that might have been echoed by those to whom such men as Van Orsdel had brought, however briefly, however imperfectly, the sense of community that religion provided: "I have never ridden it very far myself but judging from the looks of you its a cinch bet that with a horse called faith under you its a smooth flower growen trail, with easy fords where birds sing and cold clear streams dance in the sunlight all the way to the pass that crosses the great divide. . . ."

A Little Learning...

255. Rockport, Utah.

If it was men who conquered the West, it was women who tamed it, an observation often made. And with the women came the children and for the children there were the schools. A mother would put up with many things on the frontier: she would endure loneliness and isolation on the high plains, she would work herself in the house and in the fields until exhaustion drove her to premature old age and

256. Sidnoy, Manitoba.

257. Silver City, Idaho.

an early death, she would put up with life in a rowdy little industrial mining town or a dusty cow town—but she would not allow her children to go uneducated. So the schools were built, somehow. The Idaho Standard School in Silver City, Idaho [257], for example, was built with proceeds from the town's twenty-seven saloons. The buildings were usually starkly simple, the facilities primitive, supplies almost nonexistent, and the teachers frequently little ahead of their pupils in the learning experience, but for generations of children, this system provided the first, and for many the only, exposure to the rigors of education.

258. Twin Bridges, Montana.

259. Crested Butte, Colorado.

260. Craigflower, British Columbia.

261. Grizzly Bluff, California.

262. Calico, California (overleaf).

266. Freestone, California.

263. Granite, Oregon.

267. Gunnison, Colorado.

264. Florissant, Colorado.

265. Springhouse, British Columbia.

268. Las Trampas, New Mexico.

269. Bodega, California.

The One-Room Schoolhouse...

270. Cariboo, British Columbia.

The lonely little one-room country schoolhouse has become so firmly an accepted part of our shared past that it is almost legend. Yet they were real, these tiny institutions, as the photographs here demonstrate. Some, though not all, would fit the description given by Curtis Harnack of the schoolhouse of his youth: "Because each year was expected to be the last, the schoolhouse had slipped into disrepair and listed to one side over its foundation of cracked limestone. The building was about the size of our corn-crib, large and peeling-white, with sparrows' nests straggling from the eaves. . . . When a high gale blew off the flat cornfields, the loose shingles fluttered and snapped like the flag we ceremoniously raised aloft each morning. . . ."

271. Shaniko, Oregon.

273. Cowichan, British Columbia.

Little Country Churches...

Hope took many forms on the western frontier, and one of its more tangible expressions was the almost universal dependence upon religion in the daily lives of its pioneering settlers. And if they managed to build schools for their children against all odds, they were no less assiduous about building churches. According to historian Bernard Weisberger, the church was quite as important to them: "Religion had a part to play in the hard-driven lives of the frontier settlers. It was more than a mere foundation for morality. It offered the hope of a bright future, shining beyond the dirt-floored, hog-and-hominy present. It offered an emotional outlet for lives ringed with inhibition. It was a social thing, too, furnishing occasions on which to lay aside ax and gun and skillet and gather with neighbors, to sing, to weep, to pray, or simply to talk with others. The West had to have religion. . . . " And so the churches were built, no matter how small or how impoverished the congregation, no matter

274. Cottonwood, Montana.

275. Anahim Indian Reserve, British Columbia.

278. Parksville, British Columbia.

276. Chinese Camp. California.

277. Antelope, Oregon.

279. Jackson. California.

200. Manyberries, Alberta.

how much else had to be done for survival's sake. The churches dotted the wilderness, their reaching steeples pointed to the sky like arrows aimed straight at the heart of the devil. And some remain in use today. St. Saviour's Anglican in Barkerville [285] was built in 1868 virtually single-handedly by the Reverend James Reynard. A tiny, handcrafted beauty, it is now the only building in Barkerville still used for its original purpose.

281. Morley, Alberta.

283. Jerome, Arizona.

282. Las Trampas, New Mexico.

284. Cannington Manor, Saskatchewan.

287. Tres Piedras, New Mexico.

290. Randsburg, California.

293. Skeena Crossing, British Columbia.

288. Ashcroft, British Columbia.
289. Langham, Saskatchewan.

291. Bayfield, Colorado.

294. Bodie, California.
295. Lillooet, British Columbia.

292. Waterloo, Montana.

296. Fort St. James, British Columbia.

299. Telluride, Colorado

302. St Denis, Saskatchewan.

297. Regina, Saskatchewan.
298 Greenwood, British Columbia.

300. Hazelton, British Columbia.
301. Fairplay, Colorado.

303. John Day, Oregon.
304. Windermere, British Columbia.

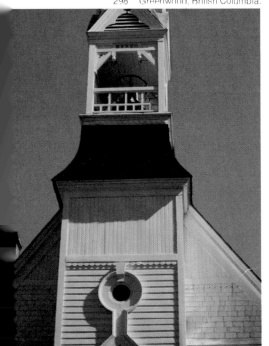

The Onion Domes...

Probably one of the most startling architectural contrasts one is likely to find in the North American West is that between the usually spare, clean, straight lines of the standard New England Protestant church building and the exotic religious structures put up by the various Eastern Orthodox sects. People bring with them what they know and what they feel comfortable with, and it was to the unlikely setting of the high plains west of Winnipeg that the great wave of Ukrainian settlers at the beginning of this century brought their concepts of church design, providing a singularly charming grace note for the New World landscape. One of the oldest of these Orthodox churches, however, was built not on the plains but on the coast of northern California: the Russian Orthodox Church at Fort Ross [308], built in 1825, destroyed by fire in 1969, and recently restored.

305. Gorlitz, Saskatchewan.

306. Buchach, Alberta.

307. New Kiev, Alberta.

308. Fort Ross, California.

310. Gardenton, Manitoba.

309. Sirko, Manitoba.

311. Smuts, Saskatchewan.

The Fisheries and Canneries

"…during that fall many hundreds of thousands of dead salmon were scattered along on the sloping banks of the river, salmon that had been thrown off the wharves because the canneries could not handle all that was caught. This, of course, was nothing new…."

Even when one remembers that Juan Cabrillo discovered California by sea in 1542; that Sir Francis Drake claimed it for England as "Nova Albion" in 1579; that Captain James Cook encountered the coast of Oregon in 1778, then explored it all the way north to the Alaskan peninsula and the Bering Sea; that in the early nineteenth century a considerable, if irregular, commerce took place from the little pinprick ports scattered from Sitka, Alaska, to San Diego, California; that fully half of those who came to California during the Gold Rush of 1849 did so by sea; that throughout the nineteenth century the Pacific Coast remained heavily dependent upon the sea for its prinicpal transportation links with the rest of the world—even remembering all that, "down to the sea in ships" is not a phrase that comes immediately to mind when considering the history of the North American West. Too much of our understanding of the West has been conditioned to such other things as vigilante mobs or cattle drives, sodbusters or mining camps.

Nevertheless, it is a fact that the West has had a long and intimate relationship with the sea from the beginning of its European history. And one of the major factors in that relationship during the nineteenth and early twentieth centuries was the fishing industry. If one stretches the term "fishing" far enough to include the hunting of whales, then the industry had at least a minor connection with the coast as early as the 1820s. The ships that hunted the great gray whale on its annual migration from the Gulf of California to the Gulf of Alaska and back began early on to utilize San Francisco Bay as a "wood-and-water" stop to rest, make repairs, and take on fresh provisions; some of San Francisco's earliest American and English settlers were deserters from such ships. After the Gold Rush established Yankee enterprise firmly in the Bay area, the connection became as solid and permanent as the nature of the business allowed; by the 1860s, the Arctic Oil Works, among other local refineries, were processing hundreds of thousands of gallons of whale oil every year.

Fish for the table was a marketable commodity from the beginning of the Gold Rush, for San Francisco was almost immediately a city of restaurants, a reputation it has maintained until the present day. The local industry was soon dominated by Italians, whose sleek, lateen-rigged "dago-boats" remained a familiar sight until well after the turn of the century as the fishermen challenged the morning sun in quest of striped bass, salmon, rock cod, halibut, and red snapper. Besides these, the Bay provided crops of oysters, netfuls of the tiny, succulent creatures that came to be called Bay shrimp, and trapfuls of crab; outside the Bay there was abalone, a delicacy which drove the otherwise respectable poet George Sterling to a famous bit of doggerel: "Some folks boast of quail on toast/ Because they think it's tony;/ But my tomcat gets nice and fat/ On hunks of abalone!"

By the 1880s, the fishing industry had expanded far beyond San Francisco. Monterey, California, had already seen the beginnings of a sardine fishing business that at its height would catch and process more than one billion pounds every year. In the north, Portland, Oregon, Seattle, Washington, and Vancouver, British Columbia, were sending hundreds of men down to the sea—if not in ships, at least in boats. Some of them went in both, as a matter of fact. These were the dorymen, surely the hardiest of a hardy breed. Every season, these men would board a large schooner and head for the fishing grounds of the far north—the Alaskan Banks—to catch rock cod and halibut. Once on the grounds, they were put forth—one man to a boat—in little "double-ender" dories to fish. All day, ten, twelve, fourteen, sixteen hours, they would fish, often in weather that left their dories caked with ice, frequently in fogs so thick that it would be impossible for them to find their way back to the mother ship in the evening with the day's catch. For month after month, this went on until season's end. Like all hard trades, this one eventually found its poet, an anonymous scribbler who penned what he called "The Doryman" shortly after the turn of the century: "I want no fuss with the pale faced cuss—/ The clerk or piano tuner—/ Who spend their lives in those stifling hives/ In the struggle for more mazuma./ But give me the wind swept ocean's space,/ Where the 'flat ones' flop in the dory's waist,/ And the salt scud whips in your upturned face,/ As you pull for the side of your schooner."

By the 1930s, the day of the doryman was in its final decline—simply because the fish were becoming scarce. By its very nature, the fishing industry is an exploitive one that depends upon a nonrenewable resource, and if the trade of the fisherman is a dying one, as many today are claiming, the roots of its death lie in the untrammeled greed of the nineteenth and early twentieth centuries. Nothing illustrates this more clearly than the story of the salmon-fishing industry.

The salmon was the first "crop" to be fully developed from the sea. Each year, this muscular beast would seek the mouths of the coastal rivers and head upstream with incredible strength, crowding the rivers from bank to bank by the millions so that a man might think he could cross on their backs; squirming and leaping, their long sides shining like aluminum foil, every fiber of their being was driven in a frenzy for the spawning grounds upriver. In such circumstances, the salmon was not fished—it was harvested. For the first few years after the Gold Rush, the market for salmon was purely local, since without refrigeration fish is not something one ships very far. But in 1864, on the banks of the Sacramento River in California, the firm of Hapgood, Hume and Company opened the first salmon-canning plant on the Pacific Coast, producing that year two thousand cases of forty-eight tins each. Two years later, the company established a second cannery at Astoria on the Columbia River, packing up four thousand cases. In 1870, Hapgood, Hume and Company began to get competition from the Fraser River of British Columbia, as Alexander Loggie and Company set up shop, and by the end of the decade five more canneries had been established on a river where in 1858 scrabbling miners had fished for gold. In 1913, the Fraser River canneries alone processed over one-and-a-third million cases of salmon.

By then, the industry had grown to astonishing dimensions. Almost no river of any size anywhere on the Pacific Coast was without a clutch of canneries, particularly in Alaska, where at Red Bluff Bay, Big Port Walter, Squaw Harbor, Petersburg, Mink Arm, Hidden Inlet, Wrangell Island, and half a dozen other places the clank and stink of cannery operations went on for twenty-four hours a day, manned by Chinese and Indian labor. When the fish were not simply scooped out of the rivers with long-handled nets, they were chased down and netted by "purse-skeiners" and "gill-netters," and from out of San Francisco, the great schooners of the Alaska Packers Corporation sailed for the fish of the north.

Why north? Simply because the salmon of San Francisco Bay had declined to the point of extinction, done in by over-fishing, local pollution, and the murky "slickens" carried down the Sacramento River from the hydraulic gold mines of the foothills of the Sierra Nevada. And so it went, inexorably, everywhere else on the coast. By 1930, the industry was tottering; on the Fraser River, for example, where in 1913 nearly one-and-a-half million cases of salmon had been produced, the annual pack had declined to only 172,300 in 1929. One by one, the great canneries closed down, their tin roofs and sides rattling now only with the wind, their wharves abandoned to dry rot.

Today, the salmon-fishing industry still survives, but only through cautious and carefully-regulated fishing. Someday, if care is taken, the salmon might once again return in the broad and shining masses of the past. If they do not, we may perhaps understand why if we reflect on the deadpan report of Thomas Kidd in his history of Lulu Island in the Fraser River: "The year of 1897...was a big-run year for salmon, and a pack of over half a million cases was put up by canneries in Richmond, and many more could have been put up if there had been more canneries to handle them. This was evidenced by the fact that during that fall many hundreds of thousands of dead salmon were scattered along on the sloping banks of the river, salmon that had been thrown off the wharves because the canneries could not handle all that was caught. This, of course, was nothing new...."

Cannery Towns...

314. Port Edward, British Columbia.

316. Port Edward, British Columbia.

315. Port Edward, British Columbia.

317. Port Edward, British Columbia.

The luckless Pacific salmon, a sleek, powerful, and supremely tasty creature, had been one of the dietary mainstays of coastal Indians for generations when the white men discovered them. By the 1890s, canneries from California to southern Alaska were processing more than sixty-three million cans of salmon every year. In barely-restrained tones of celebration, an industry spokesman from those years outlined its impact: ''In addition to the large number of canneries in British Columbia and on the Columbia River, which were employing thousands of people, there was not a stream putting into the ocean along the Oregon and California coast, which can be entered even by the lightest draught vessels, that has not one or more canneries located on its banks, forming a nucleus from which radiate the development of other industries; while along the whole coast, from California to Alaska, the business has become an important factor in the development of such sections as have heretofore been considered almost inaccessible. . . . The salmon industry of the Pacific Coast has furnished lucrative employment to thousands, and has been both directly and indirectly the means by which very many have made fortunes. . . . '' Transient fortunes, it should be added; time and a technology that rendered them irrelevent caught up with most of the coastal salmon canneries, as it did with those of Port Edward, British Columbia, whose relics are seen here.

318.   Port Edward, British Columbia.

The Boatways...

319. Celtic Harbour, British Columbia.

The boat was the basic tool of the trade, of course, and much loving care was expended in its design and construction. The Pacific Coast produced a basic design which has changed little in more than a century, as these hulks illustrate: a V-shaped bottom sharper than most, a square stern, a raised bow, lots of beam—all of it enabling the boat to ride any sea like a fat duck.

320. Tofino, British Columbia.

321. Cape Mudge, British Columbia.

322. Delta, British Columbia.

323. Altoona, Washington.

325. Astoria, Oregon.

324. Astoria, Oregon.

The Working Fisheries...

It is an old trade, one of the oldest we know. It was old when Simon Peter, the "Big Fisherman," operated a small fleet of fishing boats on the Sea of Galilee until another man persuaded him to abandon his work and fish instead for the souls of men. Technology has altered much of the trade in the two thousand years since, but its essentials remain much the same: to fish for a living means to gather your nets and your lines, get in a boat, catch fish, sell them to a wholesale dealer, who sells them to a retail dealer, who sells them to the person who wants to eat them.

327. Astoria, Oregon.

326. Winter Harbour, British Columbia.

328. Rivers Inlet, British Columbia.

329. Steveston, British Columbia.

We have always given an air of romance to this ancient trade with only marginal justification—at least according to Seattle old-timer, A. K. Larssen, who had this to say on the subject: "You hear a lot and read a lot about the romance of deep sea fishing—all the glories of wresting a living from the briny deep. Romance comes into your life under the name of Jones. . . . If it was romance, it is only a nostalgic memory today. But the fisherman himself may well be said to be romantic in that he is still the inveterate, incurable dreamer he has always been, ever carrying in his heart that cherished dream of the big haul, that big trip, that big season which was bound to find him sooner or later. Rarely if ever did the dream come true. Yet it never died . . . it never dies . . . not in the heart of a true, deep sea fisherman."

330. Aberdeen, Washington.

331. Astoria, Oregon.

332. Annieville, British Columbia.

The Railroads

"The muscle, the gold, and
the iron were ready
to make the railroad a reality."

They called it the "Great Work of the Age," and it probably was. The task was large enough—the laying of two thousand miles of track across the plains, deserts, mountains, rivers, and gorges of the West, from Omaha, Nebraska, to Sacramento, California, the most ambitious undertaking in the history of railroads, and in the annals of engineering a project comparable to the digging of the Suez Canal. It was the transcontinental railroad—the **first** transcontinental railroad.

In 1862, the Congress of the United States passed the Pacific Railroad Bill. It authorized two railroad companies—the Central Pacific and the Union Pacific—to build a railroad. The Central Pacific was to start east from Sacramento, the Union Pacific west from Omaha; at some point to be determined in the future, they were to meet and join rails. To finance the project, the government would provide a free right-of-way along the entire line, permission to use stone and timber on the public domain free of charge, alternate sections of ten-mile strips of land on either side of the line, and loans in the form of thirty-year, six percent bonds in amounts ranging from $16,000 per mile to $48,000 per mile, depending upon the nature of the terrain over which the railroad was to be built.

On January 9, 1863, a reporter for the **Sacramento Union** waxed appropriately eloquent: "The skies smiled yesterday upon a ceremony of vast significance. With rites appropriate to the occasion...ground was formally broken at noon for the commencement of the Central Pacific Railroad—the California link of the continental chain that is to unite American communities now divided by thousands of miles of trackless wilderness. The muscle, the gold, and the iron were ready to make the railroad a reality." Nearly one year later, on December 2, with similar fanfare, the Union Pacific began construction in Omaha.

Over the next five-and-one-half years the work continued. Largely Chinese crews under the Central Pacific's Charles Crocker inched up, over, and down the Sierra Nevada and entered the Great Basin, while largely Irish crews under the Union Pacific's General Grenville M. Dodge bridged rivers and climbed across the Continental Divide. "It would be impossible to describe how rapidly, orderly, and perfectly the work is done, without seeing the operation itself," an admiring observer of the Central Pacific's progress wrote, while an English reporter went to flights of fancy arithmetic to describe the Union Pacific's work: "It is a grand anvil chorus, played in triple time, three strokes to the spike. There are ten spikes to the rail, 400 rails to the mile, 1,800 miles to San Francisco—21,000,000 times are those sledges to come down with their sharp punctuation before the great work of modern America is complete."

And then it was done. In the spring of 1869, when it appeared that both railroads would be quite content to pass each other by and head off into the distance, collecting federal loans all the way, President Ulysses S. Grant ordered that the rails be joined at Promontory, Utah, on May 10. On the appointed day, dignitaries and spectators gathered at the site, speeches abounded, bottles were broken, and California Governor Leland Stanford [not coincidentally a partner in the Central Pacific] took a sledgehammer swing at the "last" spike, a golden replica. He missed, but a telegrapher nevertheless flashed the message to the world: "DOT. DOT. DOT. DONE." San Franciscans danced in the streets, the choir in Salt Lake City broke into hymns of praise to God, bells rang in Philadelphia and New York, and even Bostonians lost their composure. Speaking at the ceremony itself, General Dodge was a good deal more serene: "Gentlemen, the great [Senator Thomas Hart] Benton proposed that some day a giant statue of Columbus be erected on the highest peak of the Rocky Mountains, pointing westward, denoting that as the great route across the continent. You have made that prophecy a fact. This is the way to India."

Dodge missed the point. The destiny of the American nation lay less in the direction that led to India than in the very land over which the rails had been laid. That destiny would become clearer as more railroads began to edge across the West. And edge they did, overcoming not only the obstacles of the land itself, but also those placed in the way by financial difficulty, internal strife, and sometimes brutal competition. The Southern Pacific, purchased by the Central Pacific, marched south from Sacramento to Los Angeles, then straight across the southwest to a hookup with the Texas & Pacific in El Paso in 1882. A few years later, the Atchison, Topeka & Santa Fe, after parrying a thrust by the Denver & Rio Grande to control right-of-way, struggled down to Santa Fe, New Mexico, then west to California, where it obtained trackage rights into Los Angeles from the Southern Pacific, which had foresightedly built a small branch line to the border at Needles. In 1864, the Northern Pacific Railroad was given the charter to build west from Lake Superior to Portland, Oregon, fell into immediate financial difficulties, turned to the notorious Jay Cooke for help, was forced into bankruptcy by his manipulations in 1875, was reorganized in 1879, started building in 1880, was purchased by Henry Villard in 1881, and finally reached Portland in 1883. In 1878, James J. Hill acquired the little St. Paul & Pacific Railroad, renamed it the Great Northern, and in spite of possessing no land grants to help finance its construction, steadily moved it west [with a northern branch to Winnipeg] to Seattle, Washington, where it arrived in 1893.

In the meantime, the Canadian West got its own transcontinental railroad. In 1880, the Canadian Pacific Railroad was authorized by Sir Charles Tupper, Minister of Railways and Canals, to build a railroad from central Canada to Vancouver on the Pacific Coast. The terms were quite as generous as those granted by the United States government to most of its own transcontinental lines: an outright subsidy of twenty-five million dollars; the gift of government-owned trackage already completed west to Winnipeg; twenty-five million acres of land distributed in alternate sections of six hundred and forty acres each within a belt forty-eight miles wide from Winnipeg to the mountains; tax-free status for the company's capital, grounds, buildings, and rolling stock; and finally, a guaranteed monopoly on all railroad trade in western Canada for twenty years. The company was given ten years to complete the road, but in less than six years the final spike felt the sledgehammer in Eagle Pass of the Canadian Rockies. Thirty years later, the Canadian Northern, which closely paralleled the route of the Canadian Pacific until it reached the Rockies, completed its own line from Winnipeg to Vancouver. It followed by five years the completion of America's own last transcontinental railroad, the Western Pacific, in 1910.

By 1915, seven transcontinental lines stretched across the West, and from these scores of branch lines, some of them independently owned, some subsidiaries of the major roads, crept like tentacles into all the nooks and crannies of the land, creeping impossibly through the narrow defiles of mountains, skirting the edges of thousand-foot cliffs, poking into hidden valleys, violating the silence of desert. All the West, it seemed, was puffing cotton clouds of coal smoke, and the unearthly, haunting cry of the steam locomotive's whistle could be heard shattering the night from the Yellowstone Pass of the Canadian Rockies to the Raton Pass of New Mexico.

The impact of all these big and little lines on the West is well-nigh impossible to accurately measure. They accelerated the demise of the great buffalo herds, which led to the final decline of the Plains Indians who had built an entire culture around the animals. They enabled mines to ship ore swiftly and profitably from mining regions where transportation costs had previously been ruinous, thus stimulating the industry. If they did not create the cattle boom, they certainly contributed to it in large degree by bringing shipping points closer to the ranges on which the cattle were raised. They created towns and cities on sites that had never been anything more urbanized than a camp site. They moved all kinds of goods and services in and out, up and down, back and forth with a steady reliability that frequently brought local economies to the frenzied edge of boom.

Above all, the railroads actively encouraged and made possible the settlement of vast regions—whether those regions should have been settled or not. The land grants given western railroads in the United States and Canada amounted finally to more than a hundred and twenty-five million acres. Not all this land was arable, of course, not even in the heated imagination of a railroad land agent, but much of it was, and the railroads resorted to everything short of kidnapping to bring people to it. An early poster issued by the Union Pacific and distributed all over the east and in selected countries of Europe was typical of the sales pitch: "CHEAP FARMS! FREE HOMES! On the line of the Union Pacific Railroad. A land grant of 12,000,000 acres of the best Farming & Mineral Lands in America. 3,000,000 acres in Nebraska, in the great Platte Valley, the Garden of the West, now for sale! These lands are in the central portion of the United States, on the 41st degree of North Latitude, the central line of the great Temperate Zone of the American Continent, and for grain growing and stock raising unsurpassed by any in the United States. Cheaper in Price, more favorable Terms given, and more convenient to market than can be found elsewhere. Five and ten years credit given, with interest at Six per cent. Colonists and Actual Settlers can Buy on Ten Years Credit, Lands at the same Price to all Credit Purchasers. A Deduction of 10 Per Cent for Cash." Subtlety was not a mainstay of the infant advertising industry in those days, but the message got across and was parroted by the other railroads, as well as the governments of both Canada and the United States wanting to get rid of homestead land that lay in checkerboard plots next to railroad lands.

The contribution of the railroads to the economic and population growth of the West was by no means an unmixed blessing. Railroad corporations, like any kinds of corporations anywhere, were not noted for an unweening altruism. With little or no regulation on a government level, freight rates could be and often were juggled unpredictably to take advantage of any given situation—or individual. Substantial rebates given to bulk shippers only encouraged the trend toward monopoly to which the West was already vulnerable. Many believed that the land grants were both unnecessary and a

333. Rio Vista, California (overleaf)

criminal theft of the national heritage. Even as the Central Pacific crept toward the Sierra Nevada foothills, a critic of the Pacific Railroad Act made a loud complaint: "While fighting to retain eleven refractory states [a reference to the Civil War] the nation permits itself to be cozened out of territory sufficient to form twelve new republics." Finally, the very power it possessed to transform the land could be used by the railroad to dominate the society upon it. The Southern Pacific Railroad of California, for example, was known as the "Octopus" not only because it had put together an almost total monopoly of transportation in the state, but also because to further its ends it deliberately subverted the governmental processes, from the local to the state level, and for nearly forty years thoroughly controlled most of California politics — of the railroad, for the railroad, by the railroad.

For good or for ill, one thing is incontrovertible: without the railroads, the "conquest" of the North American West would have been unthinkable.

The Depot...

Plain or fancy, the railroad depot was once the center of a town's life, the place where the pulse of its existence was measured in the thunder and hiss of trains arriving and departing. Very few of those that have survived are still in use, and if we can imagine a ghost among these photographs, it would be the trainmaster checking his fat, round railroad watch. Will the 5:12 be on time? Will it be late? Will it ever arrive at all? Well, no, it will not. Not ever again.

337. Andrew, Alberta.

334. Pitkin, Colorado.

338. Nampa, Idaho.

335. Park City, Utah.

339. Okotoks, Alberta.

336. St. Helena, California.

340. Snoqualmie, Washington.

341. Telluride, Colorado (overleaf).

Rolling Stock. . .

The men who worked on it called it the Iron Hog, a beast that combined form and function into an expression or raw power. There was a kind of beauty there, too, for the steam locomotive of the nineteenth and early twentieth centuries was a marvel of lathed and polished intricacy, a celebration of moving parts, each one of which with its special function, each tied to each in a design whose end result was motion. The engineers, or "hoggers," as they called themselves, who operated these machines saw something of that beauty even while they respected the power it represented. They cared for them like relatives, talked to them like friends. Declared by technology to be inefficient, expensive, and obsolete, few steam locomotives are left today, and most of those that remain are cared for not by hoggers, but by people who keep museums.

342. Nevada City, Montana.

343. Heber City, Utah

344. Hill City, South Dakota.

345. Durango, Colorado.

346. Jamestown, California.

Consider these photographs and the busy life they once represented—the clamor and clang of the roundhouse and blacksmith shops of the Sierra Railroad of Jamestown, California [346 and 347]; the water tower at Crested Butte, Colorado [348], or the one at Hermosa, Colorado [352], both of which gurgled water into the hungry tanks of steam locomotives; the groaning baggage wagon at Laws, California [349]; the coal tower [350] that once fed chunks of solid fuel into coal-cars. . . . Artifacts we can invest with life only through the exercise of memory.

347. Jamestown, California.

348. Crested Butte, Colorado.

349. Laws, California.

351. Chama, New Mexico.

352. Hermosa, Colorado.

350. Chama, New Mexico.

353. Rhyolite, Nevada.

354. Durango, Colorado.

If there has been something particularly haunting about the photographs on these pages, it is perhaps because there was something in the nineteenth and early twentieth centuries that responded to the image of a steam locomotive and its train thundering across the landscape. It was the Great Machine of the era; the lyric melancholy of its whistle spoke of progress and enterprise, of muscle and money, and more; it spoke also of adventure, of the romance of the far-off, of dreams made possible and real. That sound, wailing in the midnight of the Saskatchewan plains, or lost high in some pass in the Colorado Rockies, or echoing from the canyons of the Wasatch Range, was the theme song for an age of wanderers.

355. Druid, Saskatchewan.

The Mines and Ghost Towns

"It seemed that every rock had
a yellow tinge.... During the
night yellow was the prevailing
color in my dreams...."

It is not fashionable these days to think of them as dreamers, even roman-
tics, but that is surely what they were. They called themselves prospectors,
and over a period of more than seventy years they followed a single vision
over all the rocks and hard places of the West. In their hearts was hope and
on their lips incantations, and what they pursued was, for most of them,
quite as unattainable as the mysteries of the Philosopher's Stone. Yet they
stubbornly continued the quest, enduring privation, physical and emotional
exhaustion, frustration, and an immeasurable loneliness; many of them followed the vision for all of their adult lives.

The lorelei they were chasing was that of treasure—specifically, gold and
silver. Not just money, but treasure; the distinction is important, for while
money is the stuff of civilization, treasure is the stuff of dreams—and what
we are speaking of here is a long dreaming. No one knows precisely when it
began. What we do know is that throughout recorded history the quest for
gold and silver runs like a glittering thread through the literature and traditions of nearly all cultures, strung with a filament of legend and woven into
one epic tapestry after another, typified by Jason's odyssey in search of the
golden fleece twenty-five hundred years ago. And, like most, this legend had
a basis in rather prosaic fact, for it was on the banks of the Cholchis River in
the Balkan mountains that Jason and his men used sheepskins to "wash"
free gold from the gravel of the riverbed.

As civilizations expanded, reaching out for conquest and enlarging the
boundaries of the known world, myth and reality forever mingled, until men
operated on the working assumption that beyond the next river or over the
next mountain range lay a land of richness beyond measure. Just often
enough to keep the dream living in the human mind, it came true, or nearly
true. Alexander the Great, coursing his bloody way east from Macedonia to
the valley of the Indus River in the third century before Christ, conquered
Susa, the capital of the Persian Empire, and found there gold and silver
ingots beyond all expectations; he found more in Persepolis, and again and
again piles of treasure fell into his hands before the mountains of Kashmir in
India turned his army back to its homeland.

Once implanted in history, the vision of Asia as a storehouse of riches was
never abandoned. Seventeen hundred years after Alexander, the emerging
nations of fifteenth century Europe vibrated with legends of wealth outside
the power of comprehension, and rulers of countries large and small leaned
forward eagerly to hear them, as historian Allan Nevins has written: "By

letters, word of mouth, and the first printed books, they learned with delight from Ser Marco Polo, Friar Oderic, and other travelers that cities existed with 'walles of silver and roofes of gold'; that Kublai Khan heaped in great storerooms his ingots, his masses of pearls, and his hillocks of diamonds; that Cambaluc, later called Peking, and Cipangu, now known as Japan, were seats of opulence and power that made Europe seem squalid.'' He who could tap those heathen treasures would win the world, or so it was believed. In 1488, Portugal sent Vasco da Gama around the Cape of Good Hope to Calicut, India; and in 1492, Spain sent Christopher Columbus ''to the countries of India, so that I might see what they were like, the lands and the people, and might seek out and know the nature of everything that is there.''

Vasco da Gama traveled east and returned with a shipload of treasure; Columbus traveled west and returned with an empire, for in his traveling he had ''discovered'' the New World, whose existence would change the history of Western man. What is more, he had found a land whose mineral wealth apparently justified the long, mystic dream that had haunted civilization; here, finally, was Golconda, the land of gold and silver. In 1519, Hernan Cortes landed on the east coast of Mexico, and shortly thereafter the town council of Villa Rica de la Vera Cruz, which Cortes founded that year, reported that he had encountered ''a land very rich in gold. The captain said that all the natives wore it, some in their noses, some in their ears, and some in other parts. . . . In our judgment, it is entirely possible that this country has everything which existed in that land from which Solomon is said to have brought the gold for the Temple.'' So it seemed. In 1521, Cortes conquered the empire of the Aztecs, with its ''bars and sheets of gold, jewels of gold, silver, and featherwork, and precious stones, and many other things of value,'' and found that gold mines ringed the temples and floating gardens of Tenochtitlan [the City of Mexico]. In 1533, Pizarro looted the kingdom of the Incas, the most advanced civilization in the New World, whose king had attempted to ransom himself and his people from the **conquistadors** by stuffing a room seventeen by twenty-two feet full of gold and silver in ingots and ornaments, including a silver fountain that sent up a sparkling jet of liquid gold.

Europe had never seen such treasure, and its presence imbued the New World with the magic of myth for more than three hundred years — the myth of the island of California, whose man-hating Amazons wore breastplates of beaten gold; of **El Dorado**, the gilded man of Cundinamarca, a king who ruled the people of the Columbian plateaus; of the land of Gran Quivira, a country somewhere to the north whose people ate from plates of gold and silver and whose king was lulled to sleep beneath a tree hung with tiny golden bells; of the land of Yupaha somewhere north of Florida, whose soldiers wore helmets of gold and silver; of the Seven Cities of Cibola, whose streets were made of gold, whose walls were made of silver. The myths were Spanish, most of them, but their energies powered the thought of all Europe, including that of the British. ''Bell, book, and candle shall not drive me back when gold and silver becks me to come on,'' William Shakespeare wrote in **King John**, and Ben Jonson and John Marston extolled the mineral virtues of the New World in **Eastward Ho!**: ''I tell thee, gold is more plentiful there than copper is with us.... Why, man, all their dripping pans and their chamber pots are pure gold; and all the chains with which they chain up their streets are massy gold...." Sir Walter Raleigh chased the myth of **El Dorado** almost unto death in the jungles of Central America. Queen Elizabeth I sent Martin Frobisher on a voyage of exploration to the northeast coast of America in 1576; he returned with a cargo of what he maintained was rich gold ore, and Elizabeth sent him out again, and again, only to learn that all his ore was worthless. Even the settlers of Jamestown, Virginia, had hardly landed in 1607 before they were around and about, digging after gold; in 1608, one member of the struggling little colony complained that there was "no talk, no hope, no work but to dig gold, wash gold, refine gold, load gold."

Well, there was no gold or silver for the English of America, nor the French of Canada, nor even, it seemed, for the English colonists who became the United States of America. "Gold and silver," Benjamin Franklin testified in 1790, "are not the produce of North America, which has no mines." Nine years later, the first gold mine in North America was discovered on the banks of the Rocky River in central North Carolina, and between 1799 and 1847, a mining region that ultimately spread along the base of the Appalachian Mountains from North Carolina to western Georgia produced perhaps eight million dollars in gold. It was better than nothing, but hardly enough to satisfy all the hopes that had been loosed by the Spanish discoveries of the sixteenth century. In fact, it appeared certain by then that **only** the Spanish, with their Aztec and Incan treasure hordes and their gold and silver mines scattered from Oaxaca in southern Mexico to Cerillos in New Mexico, were to be blessed by Providence with the reality that all the myths had implied.

Then on a January morning in 1848 the New World turned upside down. James Marshall, an itinerant carpenter who was constructing a sawmill on the South Fork of the American River in California [the real California], was taking his usual walk along the new millrace when he spotted "something shining in the bottom of the ditch," as he recalled it. "I reached my hand down and picked it up; it made my heart thump, for I was certain it was gold. The piece was about half the size and shape of a pea. Then I saw another piece in the water. After taking it out, I sat down and began to think right hard." After thinking, he took the gold and showed it to his workmen. "Boys, by God," he said, "I believe I have found a gold mine!" He had found an answer which generations of men had sought, and in the finding had given birth to an era during which the North American West would produce more gold and silver than any region before in the history of mankind.

During the spring and summer of 1848, the gold regions of California's Sierra Nevada foothills produced an estimated ten million dollars worth of treasure. This was no myth; the gold was **there**. What is more, a man could get at it with no more complicated equipage than a pan, a pick, and a shovel, and with no more expertise than the application of sweat. This is what perhaps three thousand California miners learned in 1848 and what the rest of the world had learned by the end of the year through newspaper stories, letters, and government reports. "The accounts of the abundance of gold in that territory are of such an extraordinary character as would scarcely command belief, were they not corroborated by the authentic reports of officers in the public service," American President James K. Polk announced on December 5, 1848, and in doing so gave the weight of authority to the gossamer of dream. The result was the greatest single mass migration in the history of the world.

No one knows precisely how many people came to California during the Gold Rush of 1849. It was at least one hundred thousand; it was probably more. What we do know is that they came from most of the nations of the world. From the eastern seaboard of Canada and the United States, where the New York **Herald** could declare as early as January 1849 that "men are rushing head over heels towards the El Dorado of the Pacific—that wonderful California, which sets the public mind almost on the highway to insanity...." From England, Scotland, Wales, France, Germany, Poland, Russia, Spain, Italy, and Australia. From Mexico, Chile, Peru, and Venezuela. From Hawaii, and even from China, possibly twenty-five thousand of those who called themselves **Gum Shan Hok**—guests of the Golden Mountain. Perhaps sixty thousand came by sea from all the major ports of the world in anything that would float, enduring overcrowding, typhus, dysentery, cholera, scurvy, fire, and shipwreck. Another forty thousand came by land, crossing the two thousand miles of the West by the Oregon and California trails, or the Santa Fe Trail and the deadly **jornada del muerto** of the southwest, or trails across Texas, northern and central Mexico, Panama, and Nicaragua, surviving exhaustion, starvation rations, waterless miles, infernos of heat, Indians, and disease.

What most of them found when they got to California was not the easy pickings of the dream. For those who had arrived on the scene early enough —or coming late, had been lucky enough—to gather sufficient capital to exploit to the full the mineral resources of the region, the California Gold Rush was a smashing success; between 1849 and 1900, more than two and a half **billion** dollars were taken out of the foothills of the Sierra Nevada by such as these. For innumerable others, the Gold Rush was, at best, brutally demanding work that might or might not pay off at the end of a day. "This gold digging is no child's play," one miner confided to his diary, "but down right hard labor, and a man to make anything must work harder than any day laborer in the States." At its worst, the Gold Rush was a disappointment of frequently tragic dimensions, as suggested by the journal entry of one Ananias Rogers, who wrote in despair from the mines in 1852: "I am solitary & alone. Am I never to see my loved ones again? If I had determined to make a permanent residence here...I might now have been well off...but my whole anxiety was to make a sudden raise and return to my family. This I undertook to do by mining. This is certainly the most uncertain of any business in the world.... Indeed I do not know what to do. Oh that I could once more be with my family. Alas, I fear this may never be. Oh me, I am weak in body & I fear worse in mind."

No one knows what happened Ananias Rogers. It may be that he did make his way back to his family. If so, he returned, like thousands of others [twenty-three thousand in 1852 alone], broken in spirit and perhaps in body. They had arrived in California young; most of them returned, like men from the agonies of war, sobered and perhaps matured by the follies of greed that had led them west. Those who remained found themselves victimized by geology; there were simply too many miners after too little gold. The bulk of the gold remaining after the early deposits had been worked over was at the bottom of rivers whose courses had to be changed to make it available, embedded in hills that had to be washed away with powerful streams of water, or locked in quartz veins in the earth, where only deep mining could get it out—all processes that required a considerable capital investment, sophisticated technology, and a labor force of respectable size. The average goldseeker had none of these, and many were forced to compromise their dreams by joining the working classes, employed by mining companies whose owners resided in the red plush luxury of San Francisco, or as itinerant laborers for farmers who had staked out sweeping vistas of farmland in the coastal and interior valleys, or as clerks and accountants for merchants who had been canny enough to keep their hands off the shovel and their eyes on the till. Others—we will never know how many—were driven to suicide or to the slow death of alcoholism and the nether world of the half-life.

But there were others who quite simply would not give up the dream that had been revived by the splendor of the Gold Rush. Jasons of a new age, these "old Californians," as well as two generations of those who followed in their footsteps, continued to wander the nooks and crannies of the West for years, and in their "prospecting" gave birth to a name and a tradition—and to the almost unnatural development of some of the wildest, most remote, most unwelcoming regions on the face of the North American continent. Moreover, many of them found what they were seeking—not as many as all of them would have liked and never again would they find as much treasure as was found in California, but enough of both to give the dream an explosive reality that would carry it undiminished well into the twentieth century. It was a performance which no other country or continent had ever seen, and one that would never be seen again.

Consider just the briefest and most incomplete outline of the remarkable seventy-year saraband of success and failure. In 1850 that saraband took the dream to the banks of the Spokane and Yakima Rivers of Washington and to the valley of the Carson River in Utah Territory [later Nevada], and the following year to the Rogue River Valley of Oregon. In 1858 twenty-three thousand prospectors carried the dream to the Fraser and Thompson Rivers of Canada's British Columbia in the north and another two thousand carried it to Arizona's Gila River in the south. In 1859 it burst out in the "Pike's Peak Rush," as more than fifty thousand rushed to the mountains of central Colorado, then in 1860 in the "Washoe Rush," as another ten thousand crossed the Sierra Nevada east to the slopes of Mount Davidson, where the great silver mines of the Comstock Lode of Nevada were opening up. In 1861 it appeared on the Powder and John Day Rivers of Oregon; in 1862 on the Kootenai River of British Columbia, on Grasshopper Creek in Montana, and on tributaries of the Snake River in Idaho; in 1863 in Alder Gulch in Montana and the Reese River Valley in Nevada; in 1864 in Last Chance Gulch, Montana; in 1865 in Bingham Canyon, Utah; in 1867 in the Morenos district of New Mexico; in 1868 in the White Pine district of Nevada and in Little Cottonwood Canyon in Utah. It came to the Black Hills of South Dakota in 1876; Leadville, Colorado, in 1877; Juneau, Alaska, in 1881; the Couer. d'Alene district of Idaho in 1885; and the Cripple Creek district of Colorado in 1892. In 1898 the second greatest gold rush in human history got under way when massive deposits were found on Rabbit Creek, a tributary of the Klondike River in Canada's Yukon Territory, and one hundred thousand people entered that ghastly wilderness to stake out their claims and the town of Dawson. A smaller rush sent seventeen thousand to Nome at the freezing tip of the Seward Peninsula in 1899. And as the century turned, the dream finally sputtered out in a few last minor explosions: at Tonopah, Nevada, in 1900; at Goldfield, Nevada, in 1904; and in the Mojave Desert of southern California in 1923. . . .

A catalogue of delights and disappointments that become dull with repetition. But it was not dull to the participants. It was incandescent with excitement, with the possiblity of yet another rich strike in the next little riverbed, over the next ridge, somewhere near the vicinity of tomorrow. And for a remarkable number of those who followed the quest, hope did in fact become truth. Virtually every single one of the great gold and silver strikes in the nineteenth century were made by men who had spent the bulk of their adult lives searching for them. Some of their names have come down to us, names like John H. Gregory, who found the dream on North Clear Creek, Colorado, in 1859; James ["old Virginny"] Fennimore, who had a share in the discovery of the Comstock Lode in 1859; George Fryer, who found the immense silver deposits of Leadville, Colorado, in 1878; Moses Manuel, who stumbled upon the largest single vein of gold ore in the Black Hills in 1876; Robert Womack, who followed the exposed traces of a vein until it led him to the first great mine of Cripple Creek, Colorado, in 1892; George W. ["Siwash George"] Carmack, one of those who first discovered the gold deposits of Rabbit Creek in the Yukon Territory in 1897. These men, and the hundreds of other lucky ones, known and unknown, were given the answer to their years of searching. Yet, ironically, almost all of them sold their claims shortly after their discovery, sold them at prices that more often than not amounted to but a fraction of their ultimate value. For such as them, the dream was too fragile to hold captive, and the quest was too precious to be abandoned for mere success; in the end, it was the searching, and not the answer, that defined their lives. Like the California miner writing in 1852, they were helpless, entrapped in visions: "It seemed that every rock had a yellow tinge, and even our camp kettle, that I had thought in the morning the most filthy one I had ever seen, now appeared to be gilded. . . . During the night, yellow was the prevailing color in my dreams. . . ."

If so many of the early discoverers could not bring themselves to hold the dream captive, there were those who could, and did. To discover rich ore was one thing; to get it out of the earth, reduce it, refine it, and dump it on the markets of the world was quite another. It was a process as complicated as the mechanics of high diplomacy and involved a bewildering variety of technological, social, political, and economic elements whose influence on the shaping of the North American West has never been fully determined, and probably never will be. Nor did it lack its own elements of color. If the saga of the dream-seekers was one of glittering legends, fabulous strikes, and great nation-shaking rushes, this second narrative was colored with the drama of city-building, of technological revolution, of high finance, of labor strife that approached open warfare, and of struggles between men whose only law was the law of power.

This was the story of men like George Hearst, a man as single-minded as a conquistador but not one given to chasing myths. With a base in San Francisco and a "poke" provided by his part ownership of the Ophir, the first great mine of the Comstock Lode, Hearst spent the period from 1860 to 1890 methodically constructing a fortune on the bones of other men's mines, buying them, developing them, and financing them through stock manipulations on the boards of exchanges scattered from San Francisco to New York, Chicago to London. The greatest of all his mines was the Homestake in the Black Hills, which he purchased in 1877 as little more than a hole in the ground and in three years had developed into one of the most sophisticated and successful deep mines in history—so successful, in fact, that it enabled him to purchase a senatorship from the state legislature of California and finance the newspaper ambitions of his son, William Randolph Hearst. Nor was George Hearst by any means alone. James C. Flood, William S. O'Brien, James G. Fair, and John Mackay became known as the "Big Four" of the Comstock; they were also called the Comstock Kings, and they went out of their way to live like kings. There was H. A. W. Tabor, whose Little Pittsburg Mine in Leadville, Colorado, produced an average of eight thousand dollars a week for more than ten years. There was William Scott Stratton of Cripple Creek; John Treadwell of Juneau, Alaska; George Wingfield of Goldfield, Nevada; and a pantheon of dozens like them who leashed the dream and gave it the muscle and direction to change the history of the West.

It was the story of industry—massive industry. Of towering headframes and mile-long tramlines, of shafts that sank to five thousand feet or more in depth, of drifts that measured their lengths in miles, not feet, of monstrous, steam-powered hoisting engines, air compressors, and Cornish pumps, of reduction mills that clattered to the thunder of a hundred iron stamps, of refineries that stank with a spectral chemistry, of mine-owned railroads that filled the air with smoke and grunted and gasped over mountains and across deserts. And if it was the story of industry, it was also the story of rarefied economics, of hundreds of owners who made their money not from the production of ore but from the calculated selling of stock, of almost constant litigation between those claiming the same mining properties, of a system of absentee ownership that included citizens of such European capitals as London, Edinburgh, Paris, and Berlin, of good mines stripped of their richest ore for a quick profit then abandoned, of frauds, swindles, and the general air of chicanery that too often characterized North America as it emerged an industrial civilization.

And, finally, it was the story of the miners—not the wandering prospectors, now, but the professional, working miners who dug and refined the ores, whose only dream was that of survival and a living wage. They came from nearly every place in the world where deep mining had been a tradition, from Scotland, Ireland, Wales, Germany, Italy, central Europe, and Mexico, but the most ubiquitous of them all was the "Cousin Jack," the Cornish miner whose growly accents could be heard from Tombstone, Arizona, to the Talkeetna Mountains of Alaska. Such men were craftsmen in a hard and dangerous trade. They worked ten and twelve hour days, six days a week and sometimes half a day on Sundays; they endured pneumonia, silicosis, asthma, heat prostration, and crippling accidents; they and their families lived however they could on wage scales that kept them at or near the poverty levels of the time—as little as two dollars a day, and almost never as much as four dollars a day. And, like most industrial workers in the latter half of the nineteenth century, they organized in an attempt to better their wages and working conditions, first in tiny unions isolated in local camps, and finally in the militant Western Federation of Miners, whose membership came to include more than fifty thousand men. The attempt failed, as mine owners, giving out with warning cries of "Red Anarchy!" and "Socialism!," brought down the full weight of industrial, civil, and military force, and for more than fifty years mining towns throughout the West rang with violence in what one historian has called "one of the most brutal class conflicts in North American history."

So was the dream captured, transformed, and—it might be said—killed. It had been born in myth, and while it flourished, it caught and held the imagination of its time and storied our history with the muscular legends of a romance unmatched in the narrative of the continent. By the end of the nineteenth century, it was all but lost in solid paper realities, seized in the grip of industry, and even the last of the great discoveries were but the dimmest reflections of something that had once inspired men to risk all that they had and were for the one great strike that would startle history and place them on a podium with all the other moneyed gods of an exploitive civilization.

And now? As the photographs that follow demonstrate with precision, not only the dream but also the industry to which it gave birth has been badly treated by the passage of time and the uncertainties of finance. During all the most active years of gold and silver mining in the North American West, probably no more than twenty billion dollars in treasure were ever produced, a pittance when compared with what the West has given up in agriculture and other industries. Most of the towns that sprouted and glittered with life in the mountains and canyons and deserts of the West have either disappeared altogether or crumbled into sad caricatures of their former exuberance. Only a handful of the great mines developed in the nineteenth century survived into the twentieth, and only one—the Homestake—remained in continuous production long enough to celebrate its centennial in 1976. There is little left now but weatherbeaten headframes, grassgrown tailing dumps, and rusting machinery.

356.   A mining headframe on Battle Mountain near Victor, Colorado (overleaf).

357. Mill of the Molly Kathleen Mine, Cripple Creek, Colorado.

359. Silver King Coalition Mine, Park City, Utah.

360. The Argo Mill, Idaho Springs, Colorado.

358. The Planet Mine in Nicola, British Columbia, destroyed by fire in 1975.

Industry and Ephemera...

In the summer of 1975 some members of the senior class of nearby Merritt High School put the torch to the abandoned mill of the Planet Mine in Nicola, British Columbia, first constructed in 1929 [358]. The act served as a kind of punctuation to the end of the graduation dance that year, and by all accounts it provided a splendid bonfire. We can deplore the fact that one generation could have so little regard for the achievements of an earlier generation, but the incident did point up the ephemeral nature of the mining business. Of all the structural artifacts that dot the canyons, gullies, gulches, mountainsides, and deserts of the North American West, none perhaps is so mutely eloquent of failed enterprise than the crumbling wrecks of mining head-frames and mills, whose broken silhouettes stand like memorials to all the holes down which money poured, only rarely to come back as treasure. "Mines are comparable to humanity," mining engineer Thomas A. Rickard once wrote. "The new discovery of a prospect is like an infant, born today, which may die tomorrow, leaving no record, not even a name. A prospect resembles a young child, rich in possibilities but hedged around with all the uncertainties of immaturity. The promising prospect may succumb to the measles of bad management, or the whooping cough of inexperience." Rickard may have been a better engineer than a prose stylist — one hopes so — but it cannot be argued that he was not dead-center correct, and not even such sturdy examples of mining construction as the two stone mills of Montana [361 and 362] could delay the inevitable; if fire could not get them, time could, and did.

362. Remains of Elling and Morris Mill near Pony, Montana.

361. Abandoned stone mill, west of Norris, Montana.

The Clatter and the Thump...

If industrial mining in the West required prodigious amounts of capital investment and human labor, it also demanded a splendid assortment of machinery—and the power to make it go. As with most of the rest of industry in the nineteenth century, the steam engine was the great machine of mining, powering pumps, mills, hoists, and air compressors. It was steam that enabled the gold dredge [363] to crawl across acres of shallow, man-made lakes, digging up bucketfuls of gold-rich earth, passing it over riffle tables so that the gold would mix with quicksilver, and dumping the waste out the rear in mounded windrows that can still be seen all over the West. It was steam that powered such ore-crushing equipment as the little four-stamp mill [364] and steam that operated the hoists that brought the ore up out of the ground to be dumped into ore cars in the ore-loading building [367]. But when there was not steam, there was always water-power, the oldest of all of man's energy sources. The waterwheel [366]—thirty-two feet in diameter and seven wide—was used to power pumps to keep water out of a bedrock placer mine on Perry Creek near Wildhorse, British Columbia, in the 1860s and 1870s [now in Fort Steele Historic Park]. The more efficient Pelton Water Wheel of the North Star Mine in Grass Valley, California [365], itself thirty feet in diameter, operated air compressors

363.   Abandoned gold dredge on South Platte River near Fairplay, Colorado.

364. Four-stamp mill, Barkerville, British Columbia.

366. Waterwheel on Perry Creek, British Columbia.

365. Pelton Water Wheel, Grass Valley, California.

368. Ore car, Crested Butte, Colorado.

367. Ore loader, Silverton, Colorado.

Where It Began...

It was in California, where the greatest gold rush in human history took place, that the almost lunatic energy began, an energy that went on after 1849 to populate some of the most unlikely places in the Canadian and American Wests. The results in California were quite the same as elsewhere, at least according to one observer of Gold Rush towns of the 1850s: "What a contrast do these funny little villages present to the eye of one habituated to the sleepy agricultural towns of other countries; built of all kinds of possible materials, shapes, and sizes, and in any spot, no matter how inconvenient, where the first storekeeper chose to pitch himself. Sometimes they are found on a broad flat with no suburb visible, squeezed together as though the land had been purchased by the inch. . . . " An astonishing number of them survived, however, in whole or in part—at least long enough to be photographed. Most of the rest have left us only their names: Jimtown, Hangtown [now Placerville], Bedbug, Shinbone Peak, Poker Flat, Murderer's Gulch, Delerium Tremens, Whiskey Diggings, Rough and Ready, You Bet. . . .

370. Former saloon and Masonic Hall, Mokelumne Hill, California.

371. General store and stable, Hornitos, California.

Washoe Silver...

They called it Washoe, because that is what the Indians called the sloping little flat below Mt. Davidson in western Nevada. They also called it the Comstock, after the immense lode of silver ore that lay beneath the crusted sagebrush desert land, and gave the name Virginia City to the town that sprouted above the lode. For twenty years—1860 to 1880—Virginia City and the Comstock Lode agitated the imagination of mining circles all over the world, from New York to Edinburgh to Berlin. "Perhaps there is not another spot on the face of the globe that presents a scene so weird and desolate in its natural aspect," J. Ross Browne wrote in 1863, "yet so replete with busy life, so animate with human interest. It is as if a wondrous battle raged, in which the combatants were men and earth. Myriads of swarthy, bearded, dust-covered men are piercing into the grim old mountains, ripping them open, thrusting murderous holes through their naked bodies. . . ." Three hundred million dollars in twenty years, and then the underground waters began to rise faster than the great steam-driven pumps could suck them out, and Virginia City, too, became just another landmark for tourists.

372. Piper's Opera House, Miner's Union Hall, Virginia City, Nevada.

373. Residence just west of Viriginia City, Nevada.

The Day of the Cheechakos...

It would be difficult to imagine a more formidable obstacle to the manic thrust of gold fever than the tangled wilderness of Canada's Yukon. But gold is in fact where you find it, and in August 1896, two Indians and a white acquaintance found it in eye-popping quantities on Rabbit Creek, a tributary of the Klondike River. Hundreds of miners from southern Alaska and northern British Columbia soon tumbled into the area; by July 1897, sackfuls of the stuff had been shipped to Seattle, and thousands of westerners from Canada and America headed north. The next summer they came from all over the world, perhaps as many as eighty thousand or more. They were the **cheechakos**—the greenhorns—and they endured dreadful privations and physical hardship as they straggled over the mountains from Skagway or Dyea,

375. Outfitter's store, Dawson, City Yukon.

Alaska, five hundred and fifty miles across Chilkoot Pass or White Pass to Lakes Lindeman and Bennett, then down the Lewes River and the Yukon to the ramshackle invention called Dawson, Yukon Territory. And then Dawson, like all the rest, was gone in the winking of a generation's eye, another town sacrificed on the altar of a golden calf whose gold never survived for very long.

376. Post Office, Dawson City, Yukon.

377. Winaut's Store, Dawson City, Yukon.

379. Miner's house, Dawson City, Yukon.

378. Mine train, Dawson City, Yukon.

380. Blacksmith and machine shop, Dawson City, Yukon.

Vigilante Country...

As in so many other parts of the mining West, the gold mines of Montana were first discovered by "Old Californians," refugees from the Gold Rush of 1849 and its aftermath who wandered north, south, and east from the state to see what they could see. In Montana in the 1860s, they found something—not much, but enough to establish such camps and towns as Last Chance Gulch [later Helena], Elkhorn, Virginia City, Bannack, and Pony, among others, all of them traditionally short-lived. It remained for the great copper discoveries of what became the Anaconda Mine of Butte to lift Montana into the pantheon of the metals-producing regions of the continent. If nothing else, the mining camps of Montana left us a residue of outsized adventure, such as the famous Vigilantes of Virginia City, who between December 1863 and February 1864 captured and either killed outright or executed by due process of hanging twenty-six members of the outlaw gang of Henry Plummer, including Plummer himself. The reputed headquarters of the Committee of Vigilance is seen on the overleaf [386].

381. Stable and blacksmith shop, Virginia City, Montana.

382. Masonic temple and schoolhouse, Bannack, Montana.

383.   Metropolitan Hotel and Elkhorn Fraternity Hall, Elkhorn, Montana.

384   Storefronts, Pony, Montana.

385.   Opera House, Virginia City, Montana.

Brighter than the Day...

387. Falsefronts in South Park City, Colorado.

Streaming West in their "Pike's Peak or Bust!" wagons for the gold fields of the Colorado Rockies in 1859, amateur treasure-seekers had a song or two on their optimistic lips, including: "Oh the Gold! the Gold!—they say,/ 'Tis brighter than the day,/ And now 'tis mine, I'm bound to shine,/ And drive dull care away." All very well and good, except that most of the thousands in the Pike's Peak Rush found what most had always found: too little gold for too many gold-seekers. Colorado mining went moribund until the 1870s and 1880s, when the discovery and industrial development of deep gold and silver ore deposits thrust scores of camps into burgeoning life, chief among them the silver towns of Leadville and Creede and the gold towns of Cripple Creek and Telluride. Some, like Cripple Creek and Leadville, survived until our own day as functioning towns. Most of the rest went the way of those on these pages, into the limbo of forgetfulness.

388. Main Street, St. Elmo, Colorado.

A White Silver Light...

At about the same time that prospectors were rummaging around amid the spare placer diggings of Montana, others had wandered out on to the Snake River Plains of southern Idaho, and here in this almost waterless country, on the banks of a little trickle called Grimes Creek, they found a flash of color in 1862. Over the next two or three years, the Idaho placers prospered, giving birth to Boise among other communities. But it was in silver lode mining that the state excelled—as long as its boom period lasted—first in the Owyhee Basin, where the mines around Silver City produced five million dollars in five years, and finally in the Couer d'Alene district of the state's panhandle, whose rich silver-lead deposits "glittered with a white silver light," according to one of the discoverers of 1885. In sixty years, the mines of the Couer d'Alene produced one billion dollars in silver.

390. Rear of buildings on Jordan Creek, Silver City, Idaho.

391. Miner's shack, Placerville, Idaho.

From Kootenai to Cariboo...

393. Ghost town of Quesnel Forks, British Columbia.

Ever since 1858, when minor gold discoveries sent more than twenty-five thousand to the banks of the Fraser and Thompson Rivers, British Columbia experienced a vigorous scattering of mining towns throughout the inland country of the province, from the Kootenai District in the south to the Cariboo District in the north. As in so much of the mining West, communication and supply were constant problems, and on the way to the Cariboo District alone, dozens of "mile houses" were built where travelers might rest, have a drink or two [and sometimes a lady or two], get fresh horses or mules, food, and supplies. Two were the 12-Mile House in Hat Creek [394] and a way station near 70-Mile House [397], a collection of log buildings constructed by the famous Basque muleteam entrepreneur, Jean Caux, in 1858. One of the largest and best-preserved [and today largely restored] of the Cariboo mining towns is Barkerville [395 and 396].

394. 12-Mile House, Hat Creek, British Columbia.

395 Back of buildings in Barkerville, British Columbia.

397. Jean Caux way station near 70-Mile House, British Columbia.

396. Barkerville, British Columbia.

Mushroom Towns...

No historian has ever been masochist enough to sit down and attempt to actually **count** the number of mining camps and towns that sprang into existence like hypertropic mushrooms during the fifty or sixty most active years of gold and silver excitements in the North American West. What we can guess with some certainty is that there were not merely hundreds, but thousands, and of these thousands the great majority enjoyed only the briefest of lives, some of no more than weeks, before fading into the dark cloak of history.

400. Back of mercantile store, Central City, South Dakota.

398. Miner's shack, Jerome, Arizona.

399. Assay office, Shaniko, Oregon.

401. Originial U. S. Land Office, Bodie, California.

402. Shaft house, Central City, Colorado.

403. Molson State Bank, Molson, Washington (overleaf).

405. Calico, California.

The classic example was Rawhide, Nevada, a gold town that boomed into life in 1907, complete with the standard assortment of banks, assay offices, saloons, bordellos, restaurants, hotels, and boardinghouses, and a teeming population of an estimated five thousand people. Today, there is nothing—literally nothing—to mark the existence of the town, unless one were to count a few fading scratches in the dry desert floor that may or may not once have been streets. Rawhide has indeed been taken by the wind. Other towns, as the photographs on these pages illustrate, left us something more to remind us of their existence, and a few remain functioning towns today, though far more dependent on what they can dig out of the pockets of tourists than anything the earth itself might offer. However transient, each of these thousands of vanished or almost-vanished towns enjoyed at least one brief moment of a fiercely exciting life, where humanity and hope boiled in constant stew of possibility, and all at one time or another would have fit the descriptions given by contemporary observers of two very typical towns. The first is Bodie, California, in 1863: "On the corner are knots of men talking mines and mining, and criticizing the specimens that pass from hand to hand. The stores are thronged with men discussing the locality and merits of the last new thing in strikes. The report of a pistol will bring a hundred men to their feet in an instant, and the saloons will disgorge twice as many more in the same moment, all on the alert to catch a sensation. . . . " The second is Jerome, Arizona, in the 1880s: "The streets are lined with freight of every description; heavy teams are constantly coming in with more; buildings are going up everywhere; auction sales are taking place in a dozen localities; men are rushing about in every direction, corner loungers are in crowds, and all is life, bustle, and excitement. . . . There is enterprise here, and money enough to build it up rapidly, and when the season becomes more moderate carpenters and masons need not be idle an hour; there will be work enough for all. . . . "

404. Sawmill, Bodie, California.

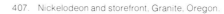
407. Nickelodeon and storefront, Granite, Oregon.

406. Wagon and blacksmith shop. Fort Steele, British Columbia.

408. Main Street, Bodie, California.

Gingerbread Towns...

One of the most persistent and endearing traits of the human animal is that if he is given the time and opportunity he will create something, somewhere, of enduring charm and beauty. Among most of the mining towns of the North American West, too soon built and too soon abandoned, there was and is little evidence of this instinct, but we are fortunate that some towns did survive—and some were born—in the splendid age of gingerbread ornamentation, or "Carpenter's Gothic," which flourished in the 1870s and 1880s. The greatest single collection of such intricate examples of the carpenter's art, of course, is strung along some three hundred miles of the foothills of California's Sierra Nevada, from Downieville in the north to Jacksonville in the south. But others can be found in a number of other towns, particularly Lead, South Dakota, home of the famous Homestake Mine, whose life began in 1876, and Leadville, Colorado, whose great discoveries came in 1877.

409. Detail of house, Lead, South Dakota.

410. Leadville, Colorado.

411. House in Black Hawk, Colorado.

412. Stoddard Mansion, Silver City, Idaho.

Always a Saloon...

No one has yet seriously investigated the function of the perfectly ordinary—as well as the more splendiferous—saloon in the life and times of the West. Certainly, among the mining camps and towns the saloon, or a collection of them, was the first thing to be constructed, whether merely a tent-shanty with a couple of boards for a bar or a mahogany-and-mirror affair with paintings of naked ladies on the walls. It was here, in an atmosphere that reeked of whiskey, beer, sawdust, sweat, and spittoons, that mining deals, politics, journalism, rumor-mongering, and even labor organizing took place, as it did in no other single establishment. But the mining saloon served another, darker purpose, as the editor of San Francisco's **Alta California** noted in 1852: "Drinking was the great consolation for those who had not moral strength to bear up under their disappointments. Some men gradually obscured their intellects by increased habits of drinking. . . ."

413.   The Dirty Dog Saloon, Campo Seco, California.

414.   Saloon in Crested Butte, Colorado.

416.   Saloon and gambling casino, Bodie, California.

415.   Magnolia Saloon, Placerville, Idaho.

417.   Table Rock Saloon, Jacksonville, Oregon.

Three Chimneys and a Coyote...

419. Rhyolite, Nevada, today.

Of all the wrecks and ruins of mining towns scattered over the West, perhaps none are more poignant than the isolated shards of brick and stone structures, for they were built with such **permanence** in mind. Now, many look like nothing more than the hulks of all those bombed-out cities of World War II, and most would match both the history and the ultimate description of Gila, Arizona, which J. Ross Browne offered in 1864: "Gold was found in the adjacent hills a few years ago, and a grand furor for the 'placers of the Gila' raged through the Territory. . . . There was everything in Gila City within a few months but a church and a jail, which were accounted barbarisms by the mass of the population. When the city was built, bar-rooms and billiard-saloons opened, monte-table established, and all the accommodations for civilized society placed upon a firm basis, the gold placers gave out. . . . Gila City collapsed. In about the space of a week it existed only in the memory of disappointed specu-lators. At the time of our visit, the promising Metropolis of Arizona consisted of three chimneys and a coyote. . . ."

418. Butte Store, near Jackson, California.

420. Stone store, Silver City, Idaho.

421. Adobe and shale store, Bear Valley, California.

In Memoriam

"The westering was as big as
God, and the slow steps that
made the movement piled up and
piled up until the continent
was crossed."

Outline of a life: His name was Ira Watkins, though for reasons known only to God and himself he preferred to be called "Harry." He was born in Iowa in 1880 of Welsh parentage. His mother died shortly after his birth, and his father put him with another Welsh family to be raised and then left for parts unknown. When he reached the age of nine, Ira's stepparents put him to work in a coal mine, and for the next five years he learned the dirty mole's life of the man underground; for the rest of his life, he claimed that those years stunted his growth. They may have, for he grew up a small man, though as tough as hemp and with great strength.

At the age of fourteen, Ira fled his loveless home and the dark hole of his working life. He found his father operating a small-town saloon, but his father still did not want him. He was shipped off this time to an aunt and uncle who operated a small ranch in Texas. Here, he learned the skills of the cowboy so well that at the age of sixteen he was allowed to trail a string of horses up to Wyoming for sale to a ranch near Cheyenne. He never went back to Texas. For four or five years—until 1900 or 1901—he rode with several brands in Wyoming and Montana as a top hand and discovered the pleasures of women and wine provided by such cattle-shipping points as Great Falls, Montana, or Sweetwater, Wyoming.

Then the urge to wander overcame him again. He went east, worked for a while as a hired hand in Kansas and Missouri, then settled in Cameron, Nebraska. There he met a girl and married her, fathered a son, and attempted to make a life on a homestead wheat farm. For two years he stuck it out, but his second-year crop was destroyed by rust and his marriage was a failure [he never talked about it much, but family tradition had it that another man was involved]. He went on the move again, returning to the grassy plains of the West. After several stints of cowboying and a period of working in the copper mines in Butte, Montana, he hopped a Union Pacific freight one day and headed even farther west.

At Reno, Nevada, he was thrown off the train by railroad bulls but made his way to the mining camp of Goldfield in the middle of the desert, where he found work in George Winfield's Consolidated Mine. After perhaps a year of work he knew all too well, he took up his poke, crossed the Sierra Nevada, and arrived in San Francisco just in time to be a witness to the April day in 1906 when the most exciting city in America shuddered and flamed into memory. For the next year, he worked as a "wheat bum" down the Great Central Valley, then joined the work gangs building the Los Angeles Aqueduct from Owens Valley to a reservoir in the San Fernando Valley.

In Los Angeles he settled down again for a time. He took a job as a conductor on the San Bernardino line of the trolley system that spread throughout much of southern California—Henry E. Huntington's "Big Red Cars." He played semi-professional baseball, did some boxing in the welter-weight class, and drank—too much, finally. He lost his job, but with wiry determination took himself up into the Sierra Nevada mountains and got work as a teamster in a lumber camp. He stayed there for two years—drying out, as he later put it. He then returned to Los Angeles, went to work as a carpenter, married a German girl straight off the boat from Hamburg, and fathered a second son. He was forty-one years old.

In 1924, Ira moved his family to San Bernardino, where he bought a half-acre patch of land and built with his own hands a sturdy, three-bedroom house. He worked as a plasterer, as a carpenter, and as a gardener for the city park system. On his land, he raised chickens and cultivated a garden that took up fully half the property. He planted fruit trees. Everything he touched blossomed astonishingly. For the next forty years he lived on that bit of ground, raised his family (which by then included a daughter), saw the arrival of grandchildren and great-grandchildren, tended his plants and his trees, built things that needed to be built, repaired what needed to be re-paired. At the age of eighty, he was still doing the work of a young man. His small body, though shortened by age, was knotted with the muscles of a lifetime of work, his hands as strong as bear traps.

But against cancer, eighty years of toughness was not enough. On October 12, 1966, shortly after his eighty-sixth birthday, Ira Watkins died.

It was not much of a life, one supposes, if a life is measured only by the size of the wake that is left behind it. Ira Watkins founded no cities, created no industrial empires, never ran for office, may never even have voted. He read little and wrote nothing, and only the tales he told to his children and grandchildren made a record of his wanderings in the West. But in his own way, in his small life, he was part of something very large. Listen to the grandfather character in John Steinbeck's **The Red Pony**: "It wasn't Indians that were important, nor adventures, nor even getting out here. It was a whole bunch of people made into one big crawling beast.... It was westering and westering. Every man wanted something for himself, but the big beast that was all of them wanted only westering.... When we saw the mountains at last, we cried—all of us. But it wasn't getting here that mattered, it was movement and westering.

"We carried life out here and set it down the way those ants carry eggs.... The westering was as big as God, and the slow steps that made the movement piled up and piled up until the continent was crossed. Then we came down to the sea, and it was done.... There's a line of old men along the shore hating the ocean because it stopped them...."

Ira Watkins never read John Steinbeck, but he would have understood the words with the wisdom of his bones, for he had lived them. And when he died and was buried, a history was buried with him. **Requiscat in memoriam**.

425. Jacksonville. Oregon.

423. Hornitos, California.

426. Wroxton, Saskatchewan.

424. Fort St. James, British Columbia.

427. Ranchos de Taos, New Mexico.

428. Alexis Creek, British Columbia.

Requiem...

Even as the ages of men are measured—as compared with those of rocks—the story of the conquest and settlement of the North American West had been a short one, however colorful, however much it had shaped the history of two nations. In that context, we might find fruit for contemplation in the words of the Englishman, James Bryce, once British Ambassador to the United States and a man of uncommon perception. He knew the West in the full heat of its conquest, and what he had to say appeared in his **The American Commonwealth** in 1889: "This constant reaching forward to and grasping at the future does not so much express itself in words . . . as in the air of ceaseless haste and stress which pervades the West. . . . Sometimes . . . one is inclined to ask them: 'Gentlemen, why in heaven's name this haste? You have time enough. No enemy threatens you. No volcano will rise from beneath you. Ages and ages lie before you. . . . You dream of your posterity; but your posterity will look back to yours as the Golden Age, and envy those who first burst into this silent, splendid Nature."

429. Stanley, British Columbia.

430. Chinese Camp, California.

Index to Photographs

Postscript

As strange as it feels to see myself described as a photographer on the jacket of this book, it is surely even more amusing to those friends of mine who are professional photographers. Most of my time is spent painting realistic, highly-detailed ''portraits'' of rural architecture. In fact, the majority of the photographs in this book were taken originally as references for future paintings. The reason that my picture-taking has been so extensive is the great sense of urgency I feel to preserve this subject matter for what I hope will be a lifetime of painting.

The creation of this book was a happy accident and, for me, a delightful surprise. While seeking a publisher for my book of paintings, **Magnificent Derelicts**, I showed the publishers of this book some of my reference slides to indicate the types of buildings I planned to include. I was astonished by their reaction to the photographs, but nevertheless dug into some fifteen thousand transparencies with glee.

The photographs in this book have been taken with a series of Pentax 35 mm reflex cameras, beginning with my old Spotmatic and going on through a series of newer models the Pentax people have kindly lent me over the last few years. Knowing little about the technical side of photography, I let the tiny computers in the automatic models make all my exposure decisions. For the most part, I use a normal lens and keep a wide angle one in my pocket. All shots are hand-held and to keep life simple, the bulk of my equipment seldom leaves the van.

I approached the subject matter with a painter's eye and, no doubt, with insufficient respect for the photographer's craft. Thus, the occasional underexposure, overexposure, fuzzy focus, fingerprint, dust, and cheap film. But this is a book about buildings, not photography. The engravers have achieved a miracle with the material they received, and I applaud them.

I now take the title ''photographer'' more seriously, and I am diligently learning what all the numbers, dials, filters, lenses, and films can do. It is quite amazing. How dearly I would like to return and reshoot some of the buildings in this book. Only problem is, the buildings are gone.

Ronald Woodall
June 1977